WEAPONS OF THE TANKERS

American Armor in World War II

HARRY YEIDE

ZENITH PRESS

CHAPTER 1

History of the Armored Battalions

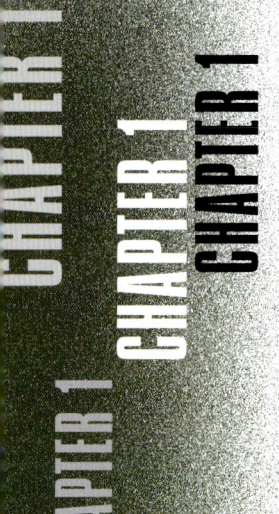

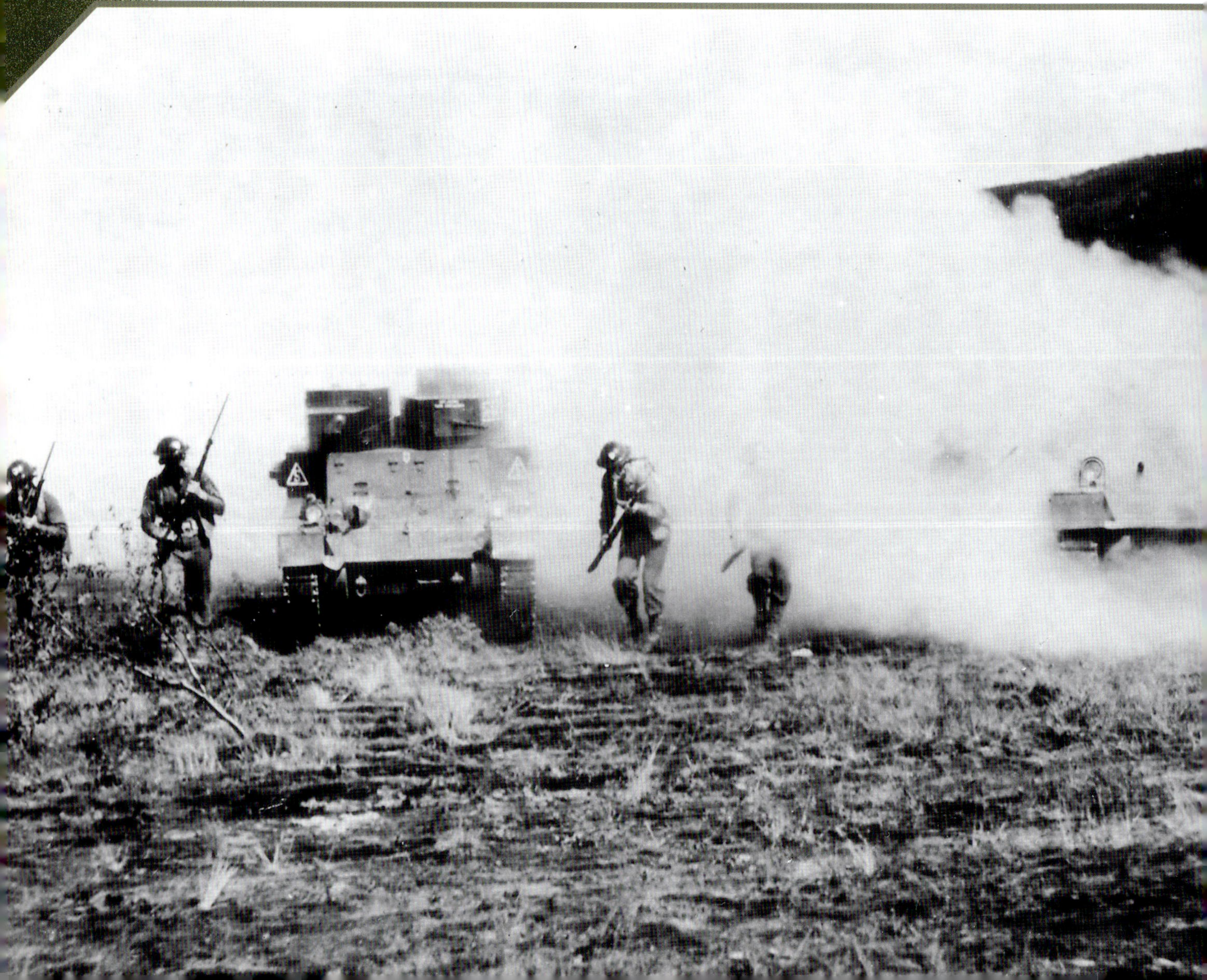

In early May 1945, the roar of powerful engines and the clatter of steel tracks announced the presence of some ninety-one U.S. Army tank battalions amidst the ruins of Hitler's European empire. Sixteen mighty armored divisions accounted for forty-eight of them, while forty-three separate tank battalions supported the infantry divisions. Another thirteen separate tank, seven amphibian tank, and twenty-three amphibian tractor battalions baked under the Pacific sun, below which the Empire of Japan fought on, unaware that it was only two terrible flashes of killing energy from its own demise.[i] Considering that a half decade earlier neither an Armored Force nor a standardized tank battalion had even existed, these facts offered both testimony to the inspiring can-do spirit of America and a sobering message to the world about the perils of rousing that people to great anger.

Indeed, it had been almost exactly five years earlier—on 25 May 1940—that Brig. Gen. Frank Andrews, the War Department Assistant Chief of Staff, G-3 (operations), had met in a high school basement in humble Alexandria,

Above: **Armor-minded cavalry officers thought vehicles could replace horses in slashing maneuver. Here, an M1 combat car from the 1st Cavalry advances during maneuvers in August 1939.** NARA, Signal Corps photo

Left: **One view of tanks emphasized their infantry-support role dating back to World War I. Here, M2A3 light tanks from the 66th Infantry Regiment (Tanks) and foot troops attack through a smoke screen during maneuvers in August 1939.** NARA, Signal Corps photo

Louisiana, with Maj. Gen. Adna Chaffee and other officers from cavalry and mechanized units fresh from Third Army maneuvers nearby. A Col. George S. Patton Jr., who had commanded American tanks in World War I, was one of those present.[ii] To date, the cavalry and infantry branches had tinkered with tanks in their own houses. They were mired in rivalry and bickering over vision—should the tank support the doughboy as it had in the Great War or replace the horse in slashing maneuver?—and prosaic matters of stature and resources. The cavalry called its tanks by a different name, "combat cars," because Congress had decreed it could not own tanks. Even within the branches, visionary advocates of armored warfare struggled to overcome resistance from old-school officers.

The men at the Alexandria meeting advocated pursuing a unified approach to mechanized development free of the Chiefs of Cavalry and Infantry.[iii] Within a month, Lt. Col. Willis Crittenberger (operations officer or S-3, 7th Cavalry Brigade [Mechanized]) informed mechanized cavalry advocate Maj. Gen. Daniel Van Voorhis that the G-3 had recommended organizing a separate armored corps that would incorporate all of the Army's mechanized formations, and that Chief of Staff Gen. George C. Marshall had approved the proposal. A formal plan reached the War Department General Staff on 10 June. Detailed consideration followed, and despite opposition to the proposal from the Chiefs of Cavalry and Infantry, the War Plans Division began altering mobilization plans to include armored divisions.[iv]

The G-3 proposed to establish two mechanized divisions, one based at Fort Knox, Kentucky, and the second at

Brig. Gen. Adna Chaffee (left), commanding the 7th Cavalry Brigade (Mechanized), watches maneuvers in January 1940 with Brig. Gen. Frank Andrews, Assistant Chief of Staff, G-3, War Department. Chaffee became the first chief of the Armored Force. NARA, Signal Corps photo

First ceremonial formation of the 2d Armored Division on 14 February 1941 at Fort Benning. Reconnaissance troops equipped with White scout cars are in the center beyond the command/radio cars in the foreground. The silhouettes of a few light tanks are visible on the far side of the formation to the left. NARA, Signal Corps photo

Fort Benning, Georgia. Mechanized units would be redistributed among them to ensure that the divisions started from roughly the same basis. The infantry's light tank formations were to be reorganized along the lines of mechanized cavalry regiments, and cavalry officers would be spread among the two divisions, where they were expected to wield strong influence. On the other hand, the new divisions inherited the organization of distinct light and medium tank battalions, a concept approved by the War Department in 1938 to meet the declared needs of the infantry branch.[v]

The Army on 14 June 1940 established a technical board to examine the material requirements of the divisions. Major General Adna Chaffee, Cavalry; Brig. Gen Charles Scott, Cavalry (future commanding general [CG] of the 2d Armored Division); Lt. Col. Sereno Brett,

Infantry; and Col. Gladeon Barnes, Ordnance, laid down several goals. All new tanks would be outfitted with 37mm guns, thicker front armor, and power-traversing turrets while development began on a medium tank mounting a 75mm gun. Diesel engines would power all new tanks (the Army picked gasoline instead). The board underscored the importance of developing multirole half-tracks and a self-propelled howitzer. It also addressed designing clothing, strengthening pontoon bridges, the possibility of mounting flamethrowers in medium tanks, upgrading radio sets, developing observation aircraft with short takeoff and landing capabilities, and improving air-ground communications.[vi]

The Adjutant General on 10 July authorized the creation of the Armored Force as a "service test," which sidestepped the need for congressional approval and allowed the War Department great flexibility in modifying the organization. Chaffee, appointed Chief of the Armored Force and CG, I Armored Corps, had full authority over tactical and training doctrine for all subordinate units and a research and advisory role in equipment procurement. The Armored Force consisted of the 1st and 2d Armored divisions and the separate 70th Tank Battalion (Medium), a General Headquarters (GHQ) "reserve" battalion. (The nucleus of GHQ was activated on 26 July, initially to oversee the training of tactical units in the States.) The units were stationed, respectively, at Fort Knox, Fort Benning, and Fort Meade in Maryland.

In a move widely interpreted as a War Department effort to overcome past rivalries, Brig. Gen. Charles Scott, the cavalryman, took command of the former infantry tankers in the 2d Armored Division while infantryman Brig. Gen. Bruce Magruder took charge of the former cavalry troops in the 1st Armored Division. Lieutenant Colonel Thomas Stark, who took command of the 70th Tank Battalion ten days after its activation, was also an infantry officer.[vii]

The initial mobilization plan called for four (almost immediately upped to six) armored divisions and fifteen GHQ tank battalions. The Army owned only sixty-six medium tanks as late as June 1940, and ramping up tank production took two years. Ordnance received a $200 million appropriation in August 1939, mostly for tank production, but only 1,467 medium tanks of all types rolled off the assembly lines through 1941. By July 1941, the Army still possessed only enough tanks to equip two armored divisions at a time when all branches—plus the British—were demanding scarce production resources to meet their needs.[viii]

The GHQ tank battalions were the stepchildren of the Armored Force from the start. The 70th Tank Battalion (Medium) initially ranked last in priority for deliveries of new tanks.[ix] Indeed, despite its formal designation, the outfit never received medium tanks and organized and trained with light tanks from the start.[x] This fact was soon acknowledged with the reclassification of the 70th as a light battalion.

ORGANIZATIONAL DEVEOPMENT

Each armored division initially included an armored brigade with one medium and two light tank regiments (three battalions per regiment); an infantry regiment; a field artillery regiment; a battalion each of reconnaissance troops, field artillery, and engineers; and service and maintenance sections. The early tank battalion consisted of Headquarters and Headquarters (H&H) Company and three tank companies, each consisting of three five-tank platoons plus a two-tank headquarters section.[xi] Service was the responsibility of the regiment in armored divisions, while separate battalions appear to have relied on external ordnance companies.[xii] All personnel became members of the Armored Force, and Fort Knox was selected to host the new Armored Force School.[xiii]

The Armored Force underwent two significant reorganizations as it absorbed lessons from maneuvers and

The first GHQ tank battalion, the 70th, was to have received medium tanks but did not because the armored divisions had first priority. The 70th reorganized as a light tank battalion. These M3 light tanks belong to Company C, which was sent to Iceland in March 1942 and later returned to the battalion as Company D. NARA, Signal Corps photo

Part of the 1st Armored Division's tank brigade in formation at Fort Knox in March 1941. The tanks are a hodgepodge of prewar models. M2 and M2A1 medium tanks, the latter with larger turrets, form the front line. They carry a 37mm main gun and bristle with machine guns. The rest are light tanks and combat cars, the most modern being the M2 light tank with a 37mm gun. NARA, Signal Corps photo

combat. The first, on 1 March 1942, eliminated the armored division's armored brigade and one armored regiment and introduced two combat commands (A and B, normally rendered CCA and CCB) under which to brigade combined-arms forces. The two remaining armored regiments each consisted of one light and two medium tank battalions, reversing the earlier proportion. Tank battalions consisted of an H&H company (including reconnaissance, assault gun, and mortar platoons, the latter two with three tubes each); and three tank companies, each consisting of three platoons plus a two-tank headquarters section.[xiv] The separate tanks battalions had a service company in addition, while battalions in armored divisions had a small regimental maintenance section attached to each tank company.[xv] The armored division possessed 390 tanks, and the 1st and 2d Armored divisions went to war in this configuration.

The second reorganization, on 15 September 1943, introduced a small Combat Command Reserve (CCR) headquarters and reduced the armored division to three tank battalions to match like numbers of armored infantry and armored field artillery battalions. The change released two tank battalions per division into the GHQ pool or for assignment to new armored divisions. Tank strength in the division dropped to 263.[xvi] The 2d and 3d (Heavy) Armored divisions were exempted because they were deeply involved in preparing for planned landings in France, and they retained the old regimental structure and larger tank complement. The 1st Armored Division in Italy did not reorganize until 20 July 1944.

The Army at the same time standardized the organization for divisional and most separate tank battalions. The North Africa fighting had shown that light tanks operating alone were generally not effective against the Germans. Most light tank battalions were therefore broken up and their companies incorporated into medium tank battalions as a fourth line company. Each battalion now had three medium tank companies (seventeen tanks plus one assault gun each) and one light tank company (seventeen tanks). Each also had a service company and an H&H company, which included reconnaissance, mortar (three tubes), and assault gun (three guns) platoons, plus a small tank section that brought battalion strength to a total of fifty-four medium tanks. Battalions in reorganized armored divisions at this time received unique numbers; 3d Battalion, 34th Armored Regiment, 5th Armored Division, for example, became the 10th Tank Battalion with no regimental subordination.

There were several exceptions among the separate battalions to this standardization:

Several outfits, including the 744th, 758th, 759th, 764th, and 767th, remained light tank battalions. They had only three tank companies plus a three-vehicle assault gun section incorporated in H&H Company. There was also a service company.[xvii]

Six battalions (the 701st, 736th, 738th, 739th, 740th, and 748th) organized in great secrecy as special formations equipped largely with M3 medium tanks mounting special searchlights and code-named Canal Defense Lights (CDLs). Each CDL battalion had a headquarters company; a service company; and three medium tank companies, each with three platoons consisting of six CDL tanks and one standard fighting tank. Each company also had two standard tanks as command tanks, and battalion headquarters had three more.[xviii]

The Armored Force starting in October 1943 reorganized nine tank battalions as amphibian tank (amtank) or amphibian tractor (amtrac) battalions and raised more from other sources.[xix] Nearly all served in the Pacific Theater. The amphibian tank battalion had a headquarters and headquarters/service company (four amtracs) and four seventeen-tank companies organized into three five-tank platoons and a two-tank headquarters section. In January 1944, the number of amtanks per company rose to eighteen, and companies received two amtracs each; the headquarters company received three amtanks. The amphibian tractor battalion consisted of a headquarters and a service company, plus two line companies with fifty-one amtracs apiece. The battalions by 1945 were reorganized into three line companies, each with sixteen amtracs. Each company had two maintenance LVTs and its own mechanics, electricians, and radio repairmen.[xx]

Two battalions, the 738th and 739th, in October 1944 reorganized as Medium Tank battalions, Special (Mine Exploder). "MX" battalions had H&H and service companies and three line companies equipped with a variety of mine clearing tanks.

The 713th reorganized on 1 January 1945 as the Army's only Tank Battalion, Armored Flamethrower. The battalion had three companies of flame-throwing medium tanks divided into three six-tank platoons, plus standard fighting tanks for the company and battalion commanders. The outfit deactivated the light tank company and mortar platoon to provide personnel for an expanded service company to handle increased supply problems.[xxi]

EVOLUTION OF ARMORED DOCTRINE

The Armored Force had a somewhat schizophrenic mission inherited from its cavalry and infantry forbearers. Beyond a substantial common base, specialized doctrines developed for the use of tanks in armored divisions and separate tank battalions, as the latter outfits had to accommodate infantry doctrine. Armored divisions included organic mechanized armored infantry elements and, based largely on experiences in prewar maneuvers, crafted approaches for their use with large tank formations.

This dichotomy did not prove to be much of a problem when units organized and trained. Many personnel from divisions and separate battalions learned their common base of knowledge at the Armored Force School at Fort Knox. The divisions evolved under the watchful eye of the Armored Force command, which imposed some degree of homogeneity in further training, and they learned joint lessons in corps- and even army-level maneuvers. The separate battalions were much more self-reliant, particularly as the pool expanded, and training was almost always conducted at company level and lower. This caused some worry in the Armored Force as "tank groups" tasked with supervising training proved unable to impose much standardization. But the situation unintentionally foreshadowed the combat experience of the separate battalions, which typically fought as company-, platoon-, or even section-sized packets attached to infantry elements. The big drawback was that the infantry-support tanks rarely had much opportunity to train beside the troops with whom they would fight, which left infantry officers ignorant of the capabilities and weaknesses of the partner tanks.

Amphibian units appear to have adopted wholesale the doctrine being worked out by the U.S. Marine Corps—which pioneered the use of tracked amphibians—through often-bloody trial and error in the Pacific. When Col. William Triplet arrived at Fort Ord, California, in 1943 to organize the 18th Armored Group (Amphibious) to train amtank and amtrac battalions, he asked what manuals were available. "There are no manuals of any type," he was told. "The Marines are starting to train five battalions at Camp Pendleton, but all they have is the Navy stuff on boat landings. Training manuals will probably be written after a study of your experience."[xxii]

THE ARMORED DIVISION

The tank battalion in an armored division was merely one cog in a big machine, and the parent organization's mission determined that of the battalion.

A light tank advances in front of a wave of medium tanks during a demonstration at Aberdeen, which reflects early doctrine for the Armored Force. NARA, Signal Corps photo

Doctrine from the start underscored the armored division's offensive role. It was to seize critical areas, envelop or encircle enemy positions, exploit gaps or breaches in enemy lines opened by the infantry, and conduct pursuit. Primary objectives would lie behind enemy lines. Chaffee foresaw that effective integration of combat aviation and armor would be crucial, a goal more easily formulated than accomplished in practice. Infantry officers, however, continued to plead for inclusion of the mission to support attacks by infantry divisions as, they pointed out, the Germans did.[xxiii]

Within the armored division, the Army at first viewed the light armored regiment as the main strike force in highly mobile warfare against strategic or tactical targets in the enemy's rear. The medium tank regiment supported the light tanks, particularly against antitank guns or mechanized forces, and could also fire as artillery as needed. The armored infantry regiment's role, meanwhile, was to break through enemy defenses before a tank attack when necessary and to secure captured ground.[xxiv]

Tactical doctrine initially anticipated that tanks would attack in three waves (and all but ignored the defense). The first echelon consisted of light tanks overwatched by a concentration of medium tanks. Its mission was to attack antitank defenses and then artillery positions, and the first wave bypassed enemy infantry as much as possible. The second echelon attacked infantry targets, especially heavy weapons and machine guns. The first two echelons engaged only in ad hoc support of friendly infantry as each wave passed through the line. Only the third echelon was tasked with sticking closely to

1st Armored Division M2 and M2A1 medium tanks pass an antitank gun on maneuvers. Tankers were at first taught to fire on and then overrun antitank guns to crush the weapons beneath their tracks. NARA, Signal Corps photo

An M3 medium tank crew dismounts with Tommy guns and pistols during training. Before the Armored Force fully realized the importance of combined-arms operations, tank crews were expected to attack roadblocks from the flanks while the lead tank engaged the enemy. NARA, Signal Corps photo

the infantry, and tankers were expected to fire on targets designated by tracer rounds.

This concept led to instructions that would only be gradually abandoned through the lessons learned in maneuvers and battle. Tankers, for example, were expected to dismount and assault from the flanks roadblocks engaged by the lead tank. Tanks also were expected to fire on and then physically overrun antitank guns without infantry support.[xxv] Both were senseless ways to expend tanks and crews.

Modeling its approach on football, the Armored Force initially created a system of pre-learned "plays" to coordinate tactical movements and firing patterns. In theory, plays could be invoked quickly as a situation developed, with orders passed down to companies by radio and relayed to platoons by hand signals. Training discouraged stationary shootouts and paid little attention to tank-versus-tank action.[xxvi] Again, experience would show that flexibility rather than plays produced success in combat, and that tanks would regularly confront enemy tanks.

THE SEPARATE TANK AND AMPHIBIAN BATTALIONS

The infantry, which had joint responsibility with the Armored Force for establishing doctrine for supporting tank battalions, also initially adopted the wave attack concept that it had in fact pioneered in 1938 and 1939. Doctrine in 1940 called for two echelons of tanks to work with the riflemen. The first would neutralize antitank guns,

while the second worked closely with the infantry against machine guns, pillboxes, personnel in trenches, and so on.[xxvii] But doctrine for the infantry-support tanks did not receive the focused attention that doctrine for the armored divisions did, and the Army did not even issue a field manual on the use of tanks with infantry until 1943.[xxviii]

Doctrine evolved in response to combat experience. The mature mission definition for the separate tank battalion as outlined in FM 17-33, 19 December 1944, was as follows:

To lead the attack.

To support by direct fire the advance of light tanks, other medium tanks, and ground troops.

To feel out the enemy and develop weak spots.

To serve as a reserve for exploiting a success or breaking up a counterattack against the supported unit.

To accompany the infantry and assist the advance by destroying or neutralizing automatic weapons and pillboxes holding up the advance.

To fight enemy tanks when necessary.

To reinforce artillery fires.

Tankers Versus Tankers

Officers involved in molding tank doctrine debated another key issue in the face of Germany's successful blitzkrieg in Europe: Should tanks fight tanks? Major General George Lynch, Chief of Infantry, in July 1940 argued "[U]narmored antitank units cannot counterattack. . . . The best antitank defense lies in the defeat of hostile armored forces by our own armored units."[i] Brigadier General Leslie McNair, soon to become Chief of Staff (and de facto boss), GHQ, that same month countered, "The [antitank] gun, supported properly by foot troops, should defeat hostile armored units by fire and free the friendly armored units for action against objectives which are vulnerable to them."[ii]

McNair and his allies ultimately prevailed on most counts, which resulted in the establishment in October 1941 of a separate Tank Destroyer Force charged with battling enemy armor. McNair did, however, have to accept procurement of self-propelled tank destroyers (TDs) rather than the towed guns central to his thinking on the subject. TDs would carry high-velocity guns to kill tanks, while medium tanks would carry the low-velocity 75mm gun that fired an effective high explosive (HE) round but had more modest penetrating power against armor. Ironically, the first stopgap TDs were equipped with the same 75mm and 37mm guns found in medium and light tanks.

Tank battalions in armored divisions worked closely with tank destroyers from early in the war. First Armored Division spearheads during Operation Torch, the invasion of North Africa in November 1942, included TDs. Close cooperation between TDs and the separate tank battalions developed more gradually, but by 1945 cross-attachments of tanks and TDs were common, resulting in de facto mixed armored units for many missions.

According to U.S. Army doctrine, the tank destroyer—here the stopgap M3 mounting a 75mm gun—was supposed to battle enemy tanks while friendly tanks dealt with other targets. NARA, Signal Corps photo

Tanks, TDs, and infantry from CCA, 5th Armored Division, work together to clear Tangermünde, Germany, on 12 April 1945. The tank destroyer is an M36, which carried a 90mm gun. The 740th Tank Battalion used several M36s in action after it had to equip itself with whatever was available from a repair depot during the Battle of the Bulge. NARA, Signal Corps photo

To assist the infantry in mop-up.[xxix]

Tank-infantry tactics evolved in response to new conditions up to the end of the war. The central question was always how the tank could best support the infantry, the reverse of the key issue in the armored division. Indeed, flexibility was so great that neighboring infantry divisions and their attached tank battalions might use completely different approaches to deal with similar tactical challenges.

Amtank battalions had essentially the same role as separate tank battalions, as at times did the amtrac battalions once they had ferried the infantry to a hostile beach. As doctrine was even less well defined, and roles changed from island to island, these battalions will be examined at greater length in the Pacific Theater of Operations section below.

THE ARMORED FORCE AT THE OUTBREAK OF WAR

The Army had few tank battalions abroad as American entry into the global conflict appeared increasingly likely in late 1941. The War Department in September ordered the 192d and 194th (less one company) Tank battalions to the Philippines. These battalions were deemed more combat ready than regular Army units because their National Guard components had not suffered the constant turnover in personnel that afflicted the rapidly expanding

Armored Force more generally and had been able to train as units. The battalions nonetheless had to draw modern M3 light tanks from other outfits before departure.[xxx] The tankers by Thanksgiving arrived on Luzon and were subordinated to the Provisional Tank Group, United States Army Forces in the Far East. General Douglas MacArthur, Commanding General in the Far East, had been unsuccessfully pressing Washington for an armored division instead. The 17th Ordnance Company (Armored) provided service to the tank battalions.[xxxi]

When the United States entered the war in December, the Armored Force consisted of the following units (note: L=Light, M=Medium):

The I Armored Corps, made up of the 1st and 2d Armored divisions; the 3d Armored Division at Camp Polk, Louisiana; the 4th Armored Division at Pine Camp, New York; and the 5th Armored Division at Fort Knox.[xxxii]

Fifteen GHQ tank battalions, including the 70th (L), 191st (L), 192d (L), 193d (L), 194th (L), 751st (M), 752d (M), 753d (M), 754th (M), 755th (M), 756th (L), 757th (L), 758th (L), 759th (L), and 760th (M). The 70th, 191st, 751st, and 754th were subordinated to the 1st Tank Group. The remainder, less the 192d and 194th in the Philippines, were distributed among three more provisional tank groups for training purposes.[xxxiii]

This was not a battle-ready force. As of 1 January 1942, the 1st Armored Division was short forty-eight light tanks, almost all of its artillery, many halftracks and other vehicles, and most small arms. The 2d Armored Division lacked even more across the board, such as one hundred forty-four light and one hundred twenty-one medium tanks.[xxxiv] McNair two weeks later informed Marshall that the 3d and 4th Armored divisions could be ready for deployment within two months only if the 1st and 2d Armored divisions completed outfitting first and gave the other divisions priority. He further assessed that "depredations" against Lend-Lease equipment would be necessary and observed that the bottleneck was not tanks, but armament for tanks.[xxxv]

COMBAT HISTORY

The Armored Force first entered battle in the Pacific, taking on the Japanese on Luzon Island, the Philippines. The one hundred eight M3 light tanks belonging to the 192d and 194th Tank battalions were concentrated near Clark Airfield when the Japanese bombed and largely destroyed the American planes based there on 8

The look of a medium tank battalion under way in December 1942, with more than a company of vehicles visible in this shot. This unidentified separate tank battalion is part of the 1st Tank Group. These are late production M3s, on which the side access doors were eliminated because they weakened the armor protection. NARA, Signal Corps photo

The 26th Cavalry, Philippine Scouts, passes an M3 Stuart belonging to the 192d Tank Battalion in December 1942. The mostly National Guardsmen of the 192d and 194th who survived the fall of Bataan joined the infamous death march, and many perished. NARA, Signal Corps photo

A 70th Tank Battalion M5 crewmember mans the antiaircraft .30-caliber at Casablanca Airport in November 1942. The new M5 had sloped armor that offered better ballistic protection and twin Cadillac engines, but it retained the M3 Stuart's 37mm main gun. NARA, Signal Corps photo

December. Technical Sergeant Zenon Bardowski, B/192d, during the air raid manned a halftrack-mounted machine gun and downed the tankers' first enemy aircraft. Private Brooks from the 194th that day became the first Armored Force soldier to die in combat.

Japanese ground forces on 9 and 10 December landed at several points, and the American tanks were soon scattered over 150 miles supporting four infantry divisions in the North Luzon Force and two in the South Luzon Force. The crews had not trained at all in their new model tanks, and fuel and ammunition were still held in peacetime depots. In just the first such tale of many, the tankers and infantry had no joint training, and infantry commanders little understood the limitations of tanks. The battalions gained an unusual allocation of fifteen Bren infantry carriers each, removed from a British ship.

A platoon from the 192d—all that could be fueled for action—first clashed with enemy ground forces on 22 December near Agoo. In a meeting engagement, Japanese turretless tanks carrying 47mm guns disabled all of the American tanks; four crewman were captured and one man was killed. On 30 December, C/192d engaged thirty Japanese medium tanks near Baliuag and destroyed eight; the tank group commander judged the M3 superior to the Japanese mediums. The tankers fought with rear guards at many points and, after suffering heavy losses, were the last to retreat onto the Bataan Peninsula on 7 January 1943.[xxxvi] Bataan fell to the Japanese on 10 April.

All founding members of the Armored Force participated in Operation Torch, the Allied landings in North Africa on 8 November 1942. Major General Ernest Harmon, CG of the 2d Armored Division, commanded a sub-task force that landed at Safi, Morocco, as part of Task Force West's operation to capture Casablanca. Company B, 70th tank Battalion, was attached to the infantry assault wave that cleared the way for CCB/2d Armored Division to land (the rest of the 70th landed later). Combat Command B included medium tanks from 2d Battalion (reinforced) of the 67th Armored Regiment. The Moroccan armored group was the best equipped in the Allied invasion force, despite being farthest from the ultimate objective in Tunisia, because its components deployed from the States and had been able to absorb new equipment until shortly before departure. The 70th Tank Battalion had been reequipped with new M5 light tanks, a rare case of a separate battalion receiving improved hardware ahead of some armored divisions. The 2d Armored Division, meanwhile, fielded the new M4 Sherman medium tank, as well as the M5. Fighting in Morocco subsided quickly, though the tankers experienced several sharp engagements against the French.

Combat Command B, 1st Armored Division, landed as part of Task Force Center at Oran, Algeria, after leaving staging bases in the United Kingdom. The 13th

The 1st Armored Division's "look" in November 1943. This M4A1 near Capua, Italy, still has sand shields, and the crew has added track sections to increase the frontal armor protection. NARA, Signal Corps photo

A 753d Tank Battalion M4A1 Sherman fires on Germans at San Pietro in December 1944, where the battalion suffered heavy losses because it could advance over only one road, which the Germans has "zeroed in." NARA, Signal Corps photo

751st Tank battalions, which left the infantry to fight off sharp panzer probes with bazookas, grenades, and ad hoc artillery batteries. The tanks were needed as over the next several days, German counterattacks came so close to reaching the landing beaches that Fifth Army CG Lt. Gen. Mark Clark considered abandoning the lodgement.

Beyond the beachhead lay the Apennine Mountains and a gruelingly slow campaign up the Italian boot. Nine separate tank battalions at peak worked with the infantry to find ways to help out in a stronghold-by-stronghold struggle. The 1st Armored Division spent months sitting in reserve, waiting to exploit breakouts that did not come.

The Allies tried to out-flank the German Gustav Line with landings at Anzio on 22 January 1944 but became bogged down in an extended siege by German forces holding the high ground around the beachhead. The 1st

Mountainous terrain often relegated tanks to indirect-fire missions. Here, M4s from the 755th Tank Battalion fire as artillery near Pietramala, Italy, on 1 October 1944. NARA, Signal Corps photo

Armored Division (less CCB) was shifted to Anzio shortly after the landings, but its tank battalions spent most of the time dug in to a pine forest firing artillery missions until the breakout for Rome in May (liberated on 4 June). Moreover, at the time of the spring offensive in 1944, Headquarters, Mediterranean Theater of Operations, still found general agreement among Fifth Army units "that there has been a definite lack of coordination and teamwork vitally necessary. . ., particularly between infantry and tanks."

One key problem was the frequent reattachment of separate tank battalions to unfamiliar infantry commands. "My battalion was attached so many times that I almost lost count," complained the CO of the 756th Tank Battalion. "In one case, the battalion was attached to three different organizations within a period of twelve hours."

Attacking skilled German defenders who held the excellent defensive ground amply provided by Italy tended to produce high casualties. During the Anzio breakout, for example, the 191st Tank Battalion suffered such crippling losses that the 34th Infantry Division had to substitute its attached tank destroyer battalion as assault guns.

American formations in 1944 found that under the conditions prevailing in Italy, the most effective way to use tanks and infantry was to assault using medium tanks, followed at approximately one to two hundred yards by infantry closely supported by light tanks. This stood early tank doctrine on its head.

There appears to have been no meaningful difference between the way the separate tank battalions and those in the 1st Armored Division worked with either armored or regular infantry. This is not surprising as the armored division rarely performed the mission of rapid maneuver or exploitation envisioned by doctrine. Fifth

755th Tank Battalion medium and light tanks in Coreno, Italy, just after its capture on 14 May 1944. The M4 exhibits first-generation characteristics in nearly every respect, although it has appliqué armor over the gunner's position. NARA, Signal Corps photo

Army added to doctrine during the spring 1944 offensive, when it used tank-borne infantry on a large scale for the first time in American practice. The 1st Armored Division and the tank battalions did finally get to run a bit during the final breakout to the Alps in April 1945.

Tank battalion equipment took another step forward in Italy, where the M5 had supplanted the M3 in light tank companies. The M8 assault gun replaced the T30 in tank battalions, soon to be supplanted in turn by the 105mm Sherman in standard tank battalions. Mine clearing Scorpion tanks, which beat the earth with chains attached to a spinning drum, were used for the first time.

EUROPEAN THEATER OF OPERATIONS (ETO)

The war in Northwest Europe after D-day, 6 June 1944, was the main field of battle for the Armored Force. Every armored division except for the 1st fought there, as did most of the Army's separate tank battalions.

Dependence on the infantry to clear landing areas for tanks in Sicily and Italy had weakened the assault waves' ability to handle counterattacks, and commanders determined that the doughs would enjoy close tank support on the Normandy beaches. Three separate battalions—the 70th, 741st, and 743d—received new highly secret equipment to accomplish that mission: duplex drive (DD) amphibious Shermans. Two companies from each battalion were scheduled to land moments ahead of the infantry assault wave. The 70th landed at Utah Beach with few complications; the 741st lost most of its DD tanks off

A tank dozer clears obstacles on Omaha Beach on D-Day. Three separate tank battalions—the 70th, 741st, and 743d—participated in the assault wave on the two American beaches. Coast Guard photo, National Archives

A knocked-out DD tank, probably on Omaha Beach. Spotty photographic evidence, including Robert Capa's famous pictures from Omaha, indicates that crews under fire fully collapsed only the front of their screens so that they could shoot. NARA, Signal Corps photo

Omaha Beach in heavy seas, while nearby the 743d rode its assault craft to shore rather than risk the sea conditions. The tanks made a key contribution, particularly at Omaha Beach, where the operation was touch-and-go for many hours.

Established doctrine went out the window as infantry and tankers grappled with difficulties posed by the Norman hedgerows, and together they worked out a new way to fight. Ubiquitous German use of "bazookas" such as the panzerfaust, for example, meant that sending any tank wave ahead of the infantry spelled disaster. The two arms had to work together intimately—and with others such as the engineers and artillery— to minimize losses for both. The period was mainly a story of the separate tank battalions, although the 2d and 3d Armored divisions became embroiled too.

Neither the tankers nor infantry were prepared for the demands of vicious hedgerow fighting, which started just beyond the beaches. Here, heavily camouflaged Shermans from the 70th Tank Battalion support the 8th Infantry Regiment, 4th Infantry Division, northwest of St. Lô on 23 July 1944. NARA, Signal Corps photo

The big armor's turn came with the Operation Cobra breakout in late July. Armored divisions fulfilled the wildest dreams of the armored warfare visionaries as they slashed, encircled, and spearheaded a drive clear across France to the German border by mid-September. The mechanical reliability central to American tank design paid off handsomely, and some tanks drove all the way from the beaches to central Germany without any major mechanical failures. DD tanks assigned to separate tank battalions—the 191st, 753d, and 756th—supported the landings in southern France on 15 August.

Tank battalions adopted new techniques in the hedgerows. A 709th Tank Battalion M5A1 in July 1944 has sandbags for extra armor protection and the Culin hedgerow-busting device that allowed tanks to plow through the obstructions. NARA, Signal Corps photo

Only in Lorraine, France, beginning on 19 September was there a major tank fight. There, the fresh 111th and 113th Panzer brigades and then the 11th Panzer Division attacked CCA/4th Armored Division. Now battle-wise Sherman and TD crews through maneuver and superior position destroyed dozens of Panthers before the Germans broke off the operation.

The fighting along the German border again all but erased the difference between the separate and divisional tank battalions. It was smash-mouth combined-arms

A Panther rolls toward Luneville during the counterattack against Patton's Third Army in Lorraine. The Mark V outclassed even late-production Shermans in fire power and armor, but it was mechanically less reliable, weighed half again as much, and consumed more fuel. National Archives, German newsreel

Tanks blast German infantry near Gelim, Belgium, on 3 September 1944 as Allied forces drive toward the Siegfried Line. The tank to the right is an M4A1 (76mm), which provided the commander with a vision cupola and single-piece hatch. The tank's rubber chevron tracks show the heavy wear inflicted by the long race from Normandy. An M4 with its split commander's hatch and rubber block tracks is to the left. NARA, Signal Corps photo

Shermans and M36s with the 7th Armored Division during fighting near St. Vith in January 1945. Tankers often turned to the tank destroyers to handle heavy German tanks because their own guns lacked the penetrating power. National Archives, Signal Corps photo

A Sherman crosses the Rhine River on the Remagen Bridge, which was captured intact after a dashing drive by the 9th Armored Division on 7 March 1945.
NARA, Signal Corps photo

A 707th Tank Battalion M4A3 (76mm) fires at a building outside Bamberg in support of the 89th Infantry Division's advance on the city in April 1945. The steel frame visible on the hull was added by Service Company to hold sandbags but is now empty.
NARA, Signal Corps photo

An M4A3 (76mm) from the 22d Tank Battalion, 11th Armored Division, has just fired a white phosphorous round into a house while clearing Wernberg, Germany, on 22 April 1945. Riflemen from the 55th Armored Infantry Battalion race past the tank. NARA, Signal Corps photo

fighting against resurgent German defenses in West Wall fortified lines and in cities. At Puffendorf on 16 November, King Tigers and Panthers from the 9th Panzer Division mauled two tank battalions of the 2d Armored Division, a reminder that tank-for-tank, the Sherman was outmatched by heavy panzers in slugging matches.

The German Ardennes offensive beginning 16 December again tested American armor on the defense. Kasserine Pass was a distant memory, and American tankers mainly held where they had to, even when outnumbered: the 7th Armored Division at St. Vith, the 741st Tank Battalion at Rocherath, the 70th Tank Battalion on the southern shoulder. The tank battalions played their role in the counterstrike, and the Germans were driven from the Bulge having suffered irreparable losses.

The Americans crossed the Roer River in late February 1945, the first step in a cascading wave of motion that in March destroyed the German armed forces west of the Rhine River and then leapt that formidable stream. By VE Day, American armored spearheads had rolled as far as the east bank of the Elbe River, Czechoslovakia, and Austria.

The ETO spawned a tremendous variation in tank battalion equipment in response to evolving needs. Dozer tanks came ashore on D-day and played roles from plowing up mines to busting hedgerows to burying pillboxes. Culin hedgerow cutters, the brainchild of a creative sergeant, gave American tanks movement superiority in hitherto German-friendly terrain. Jumbo assault tanks appeared, and many Shermans were issued with a higher velocity 76mm gun. Flamethrowers were put into Shermans, and rocket launchers on top of them. Mine clearing tanks went into action. Amtracs appeared and the DD Sherman reappeared for river crossings. Finally, a few battalions received the new M24 light tank, while others in the 3d and 9th Armored divisions got a handful of M26 heavy tanks, thought to be a match for the Tiger. Even the CDL Lee tank got a brief moment in the spotlight illuminating river-bridging operations.

A Sherman tank, probably belonging to the 754th Tank Battalion, leads attacking 37th Infantry Division riflemen with fixed bayonets on Bougainville on 16 March 1944. NARA, Signal Corps photo

PACIFIC THEATER

Armor operated on a much more limited scale in the Pacific than in Europe, but some campaigns fielded as many tanks as were used in North Africa. Two separate tank battalions participated in the Central Pacific campaign, two joined fought in the Northern Solomons, three soldiered in the Bismarck Archipelago and Eastern Mandates, and five fought on New Guinea and in the Western Pacific. Twelve fought in the Philippines, and the Ryukyu campaign, including Okinawa, involved eight. Rather than describe a string of generally similar island campaigns, the section relates how armored battalions fought in the theater.

Specialized battalions played a substantially larger role than they did in North Africa or Europe, particularly amphibian units. U.S. Army amtanks and amtracs first entered battle during landings on Kwajalein beginning 31 January 1944, when the 708th Provisional Amphibian Tractor Battalion (the temporarily reorganized 708th Amphibian Tank Battalion less Company D plus three infantry antitank companies converted to LVTs) landed

with the 7th Infantry Division. Company A of the 708th went into battle in LVT(A)(1) amtanks, while other elements used LVT(A)(2) or LVT(2) amtracs.

During amphibious landings, the usual approach was to use a lead wave of amtanks followed by waves of amtracs at one-to-three minute intervals, although some units instead put amtanks on the flanks and interspersed a few among the amtracs. In either case, only the first wave came in firing. A post-war survey indicated that the leading causes of vehicle losses were rough surf and mechanical deadlining, while losses to enemy action ranged from only 5 percent to 50 percent, depending on unit.[xl] Army amphibian battalions at times supported

M3 Lees just after the collapse of Japanese resistance on Makin Atoll, Central Pacific, on 24 November 1943. This was the last combat appearance of the Lee in American service. NARA, Signal Corps photo

View from a Water Buffalo during the 7th Infantry Division assault landing on Enubuj Island, Kwajalein, on 2 February 1944. The infantry transported on board the LVT helped man the machine guns during the run into the beach. NARA, Signal Corps photo

This is how waves of LVTs heading toward the beach looked from the air, in this case **Marine Corps assault troops landing on Iwo Jima.** U.S. Navy photo

Marine Corps elements, and their Marine counterparts at times worked with Army formations.

Amphibian tanks supported the infantry at the waterline and during the initial push beyond the beach. They would often lead infantry attacks against Japanese machine-gun nests and bunkers, as enemy fire generally consisted of small arms, mortar, and artillery rather than antitank. Nonetheless, commanders who exposed themselves to see ran a high risk of being shot, and vehicle losses to mortar and artillery were fairly common.[xli] A secondary mission for amtanks armed with the 75mm howitzer was to provide artillery support to the infantry until divisional artillery came ashore; a battalion had the same number of howitzers, albeit lighter ones, as did divisional artillery. On Leyte in the Philippine Islands, after the initial landings on 20 October 1944, 776th Amphibian Tank Battalion amtanks accompanied by amtracs from the 718th and 536th Amphibian Tractor battalions conducted water reconnaissance and amphibian raids into the enemy's rear area, where they shot up supply installations, gun positions, and troop concentrations. Water marches of up to 117 miles characterized such operations.[xlii]

Typical amphibian tractor battalion missions, meanwhile, included carrying assault infantry to the beach, crossing rivers, reconnaissance, spearheading infantry attacks, attacking machine-gun nests, and mopping-up operations. Once a beachhead was established, amtracs brought supplies forward, evacuated wounded troops, conducted ship-to-shore operations, and laid communication wires.

Water-proofed standard tanks (called "land tanks" by amphibian units) with wading gear followed the assault wave ashore from landing craft, and the standard tank battalions with their heavier guns and armor took over most of the tank work. Amtanks and amtracs nonetheless

An LVT(A)(4) from the 708th Amphibian Tank Battalion supports Tenth Army troops taking cover from heavy fire before advancing into Zamami Shima in the Ryukyu Islands on 26 March 1945. NARA, Signal Corps photo

A 708th Amphibian Tank Battalion LVT(A)(1), which was the first type of amtank produced, works inland with the 77th Infantry Division on Keise Shima on 31 March 1945. NARA, Signal Corps photo

An LVT(2) crew watches the brush off Red Beach on Butaritari Island, Makin Atoll, in November 1943; the .50-caliber has just been fired at something as it is smoking. The amtrac wielded a tremendous amount of automatic weapons fire power that could help out the infantry. NARA, Signal Corps photo

continued to work with the land tanks and the infantry against enemy positions inland. The 780th Amphibian Tank Battalion after the Leyte landings had to fight with the infantry several miles into the interior over five days because the ground was too swampy for land tanks to move forward.[xliii]

Fragmentation of the separate tank battalions was extreme in the Pacific as compared with other theaters. A post-war report noted that only a single battalion remained

Water-proofed 767th Tank Battalion M4A1s with wading gear land with the 7th Infantry Division on Kwajalein on 2 February 1944. The forward stack was for the air intake, and the rear one handled exhaust. NARA, Signal Corps photo

Action was usually at close range in the Pacific Theater. Here, an M3 on Bougainville sits almost atop a Japanese bunker that has just been worked over by a flamethrower. NARA, Signal Corps photo

attached to the same division throughout hostilities, and that attachments typically broke units up into company- and even platoon-sized packets assigned to divisions.[xliv]

Combat conditions were markedly different from those in North Africa and Europe. Terrain was usually exceedingly rough; tanks operated on narrow, steep roads and at times required help from tractors to move into position. Close-in vision from inside a buttoned up tank was so restricted that a common expedient was to direct the maneuver of a tank by radio from a second tank with a better view. In one case, a tank backed two miles down a mountain trail under such guidance. Some units patched together extended periscopes for commanders by fastening two together.

Tanks engaged almost entirely in assault firing and almost never acted as reinforcing artillery. Action was generally close-in against numerous, well-concealed defensive positions, and ranges were usually less than 500 yards and often less than a hundred. Good gunnery was at a premium as rounds had to be aimed at small firing slits or cave mouths, and blasting away cover and knocking out bunkers demanded high rates of fire and ammunition consumption.

On the bright side, total casualties in Pacific Theater tank units were quite light and generally involved commanders shot through the head or personnel outside

Tanks and riflemen from the 40th Infantry Division assault Japanese positions on Panay, Philippine Islands, on 18 March 1945. Note the fixed bayonet, a sure sign of close-quarters action. NARA, Signal Corps photo

the tanks. The shortage of Japanese AT guns and heavy artillery resulted in few serious wounds or burns to tank crews. (The 47mm high-velocity antitank gun earned respect when it did appear, as it could hole a Sherman's frontal armor from 500 yards.) Indeed, unlike in other theaters, an Army survey found that crews did not fear fires breaking out in their tanks.[xlv]

Tank battles were rare, and as the war progressed, American units encountered Japanese tanks in the open with ever decreasing frequency; the enemy opted instead to dig tanks in as pillboxes.[xlvi] The Sherman outclassed Japanese tanks in fire power and armor, and light tanks and even amtanks could hold their own. The M4 also enjoyed superior mobility in muddy terrain, according to field reports.[xlvii]

Light Tanks

The light tank moved from the center of America's mechanized warfare scheme to a virtual noncombatant during the first five years of the Armored Force. The infantry light tanks and cavalry combat cars produced in the late 1930s were nearly identical to one another in many respects, both being built at Rock Island Arsenal. Hull layouts were the same, although the infantry versions had slightly heavier armor. The Combat Car M1 (redesignated the light tank M1A2 in 1940), for example, had front armor 5/8-inch thick, while the infantry had boosted the armor on its M2A3 light tank to 7/8-inch thickness. The bogie-wheel-based vertical volute spring suspension systems were the same, and both used the 250-horsepower Continental radial aircraft engine. Machine guns provided the armament, while four men crewed each.

The infantry nonetheless had taken the extra step of arming the M2A4 light tank with a 37mm gun in 1939. Still in thrall to the idea that a tank should throw as much lead as possible—aimed or not—two machine guns were mounted in the side sponsons for use by the driver. The front armor was thickened to 1 inch. Considering that the contemporaneous German Panzerkampfwagen III Ausf. D medium tank (always called the Mark III by American tankers) had nearly identical characteristics, the American light tank had become fairly muscular by global standards. Indeed, although deemed obsolete by the Army, the Marine Corps used the M2A4 in combat early in the war.

The M2A4 being demonstrated at Aberdeen Proving Ground in October 1939. The tank was the rough equal of the lightest German medium tank at that time. Note the commander's pre-war "donut-style" crash helmet. NARA, Signal Corps photo

Above: **The Combat Car M1/Light Tank M1A2 weighed nearly ten tons and carried one .50-caliber and one .30-caliber machine gun in the turret, plus a .30-caliber in the hull.** NARA, Signal Corps photo

Left: **The M2A3 had slightly thicker armor than the M1 combat car and split its upper machine guns between two turrets so that gunners could engage more targets simultaneously. These belong to the 66th Infantry Regiment (Tanks).** NARA, Signal Corps photo

The 37mm gun breach and guard in the turret of a museum-preserved M3A1 tank. The loader's seat is visible at the top of the picture. Carlos Caceres

This M3A1 is escorting a truck convoy near Maknassy, Tunisia, on 8 April 1943. This shot offers a view of the turret top, which now provides egress to both commander and loader. The tank has a typical air-recognition white star painted on the turret top. NARA, Signal Corps photo

This late-production M3A1, which is being "mined" during an exercise, has a welded hull. Note the absence of the sponson machine guns and turret cupola. Library of Congress, Prints & Photographs Division, FSA-OWI Collection

The M3 series served on in the Pacific long after it had been retired elsewhere. These M3A1 Stuarts are still in action with the 754th Tank Battalion on 9 March 1944. They are moving forward to attack Japanese pillboxes on Bougainville's Hill 700. NARA, Signal Corps photo

tion, and the FM radio was upgraded to the SCR-508. The weight climbed slightly to over 14 tons.

Another model, the M3A3, was introduced in August 1942 for Lend-Lease but was not used by the American tank battalions. It strongly resembled the M5 light tank but lacked the characteristic hump at the back of the deck. The M3 was declared obsolete in July 1943 and the M3A1 one year later.

Early fighting in North Africa suggested that the light tank could play the full-fledged armored role written for it in doctrine. Lieutenant Colonel John Waters commanded 1/1st Armored Regiment, 1st Armored Division, which landed equipped with M3s at Oran, Algeria on 8 November 1942 attached to the 13th Armored Regiment. A day later, one of his companies supported by TDs knocked out fourteen French light tanks for the loss of

The pilot version of the M5 (M3 Experimental) had a fixed hull-mounted machine gun in addition to the one in the ball mount. The sloped front armor provided better protection than the slab-fronted M3, and the hull crew enjoyed overhead hatches with rotating periscopes. NARA, Signal Corps photo

It is no good for tank-versus-tank combat." Indeed, the word from all corners was that the 37mm gun was worthless against enemy tanks except for hard-to-get shots at the sides and rear from well under a thousand yards.

M5 STUART

The M5 light tank was initially designed as a modification of the M3A1 using a modern armor layout, twin Cadillac engines, and a Hydra-Matic transmission, which provided automatic gear shifting. The new design was standardized in February 1942.

A comparison of the new M5 (left) and several M3A1s with welded hulls. The dual V-8 Cadillac engines in the M5 were the most important improvement. NARA, Signal Corps photo

one M3. The battalion engaged German armor at Chouigui Pass, Tunisia, on 25 November. Waters told a military observer, "At 0830 some German tanks appeared on the scene. We were sitting pretty for them. We did not have to move as one platoon of tanks guarded the pass behind the hill and one platoon [was] on the other side. Another platoon was situated on the other side of the road in a gully when the German tanks advanced down the road, six Mark IVs and three Mark IIIs. They got within three hundred yards of the platoon on the hill when it opened up on the German tanks. The going was pretty tough stopping them, and I ordered another company and assault guns in and destroyed six Mark IVs and one Mark III. We lost six tanks doing it. . . . After that battle, we really thought our light tank was a good tank."

Waters added in a series of random notes he jotted down on 31 December, "The light tank (M3A1) is pound for pound and gun for gun an outstanding vehicle. It held its own against the Mark IV Special when not out-ranged [300 yards against the Mark IV's side armor] and when able to ambush the German vehicle."

There nevertheless were dire portents despite the successful outcome at Chouigui Pass. One M3 crew during the action fired eighteen 37mm rounds at the front of a Mark IV to no effect before the panzer casually annihilated the little tank with a 75mm blast. By January 1943, Lt. Col. E. A. Russell, executive officer of CCB, 1st Armored Division, flatly told an observer, "The [M3] light tank is excellent for reconnaissance in force, exploitation, and wide harassing attacks and hit-and-run attacks.

The first M5 light tanks fielded in action belonged to the 70th Tank Battalion, here seen parading for President Franklin Roosevelt at Casablanca in January 1943. NARA, Signal Corps photo

A look at the deck of the M5. These tanks have a triangular commander's hatch, which proved a difficult squeeze for any large man and were replaced on later models with more spacious hatches. NARA, Signal Corps photo

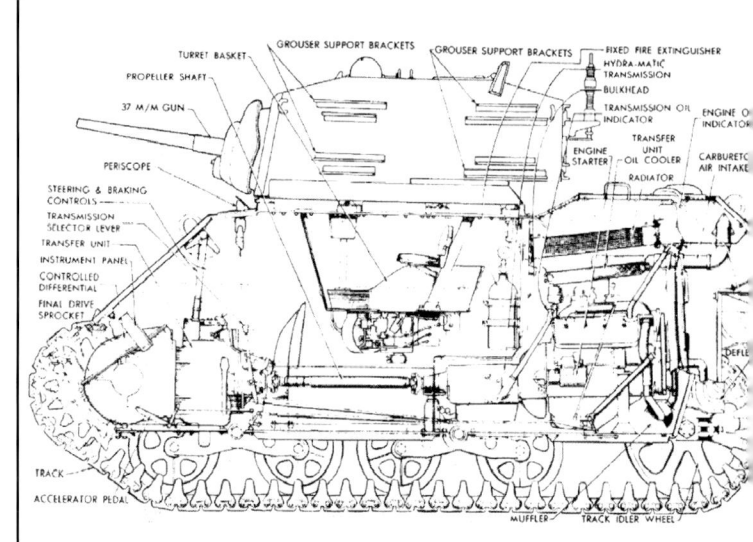

A cut-away view of the M5A1 light tank. U.S. Army

The all-welded hull had 1-1/8-inch sloped upper frontal armor in place of the old slab configuration, which provided the ballistic protection of 2-1/2 inches. Armor on the sides and rear was up to 1-1/8 inches thick, and the turret had 1-3/4 inches on the front and 1-1/4 inches on the sides and rear. The driver and bow gunner now enjoyed the convenience of overhead hatches equipped with periscopes.

The M5 retained the 37mm main gun and coaxial .30-caliber machine gun, and the bog retained a .30-caliber machine gun in a hull ball mount. The turret had a basket, and the fighting compartment was somewhat roomier than in the M3 because the drive train ran closer to the

The turret basket on an M5A1; the basket on the M3A1 and M5 looked about the same. The vehicle to the right is an M32 tank retriever. NARA, records of the Chief of Ordinance

An M5, likely from the 1st Armored Division, fires during action in Tunisia in early 1943. The day of the light tanks as real battle tanks were over, and henceforth they generally played a supporting role in the war against Germany. NARA, Signal Corps film

floor. The crew could traverse the turret using either a hydraulic or manual mechanism. The vehicle had organized stowage for one hundred twenty-three 37mm shells and 6,250 .30-caliber rounds.

The tank was outfitted with a one-cylinder auxiliary generator, often called the "little Joe," to charge the batteries, which the radio drained if used when the main engine was not running. The vehicle had an interphone system and was fitted with an FM radio model SCR-508, -528, or –538; command tanks had an additional SCR-506 AM radio.

A look at the upper surfaces of the M5A1, courtesy of a German antitank mine. Note the improved hatch arrangement in the extended turret. The white line is tape marking the mined area. NARA, Signal Corps photo

A rear view of an M5A1 laden with the usual bedrolls and other personnel crew gear. This is the first tank to cross the Volturno River via "Huskie Bridge" on 13 October 1944. NARA, Signal Corps photo

A stabilizer was fitted to the main gun, but crews never thought much of the gyrostabilizer on this or any other American tank model during the war. Captain Atlee Wampler, who in March 1943 took command of A/70th Tank Battalion in Tunisia, said of the gyrostabilizer, "When on the move and bouncing up and down, you were looking at the sky, then the ground. So we learned the hard way in Tunisia that we needed someone in position to fire, to cover other tanks when we moved."[l] A post-war survey of tank crewmen who served in all models indicated that they almost never used the gyrostabilizer in battle.[li]

The twin eight-cylinder Cadillac engines delivered 220 horsepower at 4,000 revolutions per minute, and the M5 could travel at 36 miles per hour on level ground. The vehicle carried 89 gallons of gasoline and had a cruising range of 100 miles.

The M5A1 was standardized in September 1942, the chief modification being a turret that had a bulge at the rear to hold the radio. A new combination gun mount incorporated a direct 3-power gun sight, and the antiaircraft machine gun was moved to a mount on the turret side. The commander's position had both a new 360-degree periscope and an additional rear-facing periscope.

Crew escape options were improved, which was a gift to men who had to crew a vehicle that appeared ever more fragile as compared with the increasingly lethal guns and heavier tanks on the European battlefield. The hatches were enlarged all around, and a new escape hatch was incorporated in the hull floor. The adjusted

Dog Company, 709th Tank Battalion, light tanks in Kleinhau, Germany. A late-production M5A1, recognizable by a shield covering the machine gun mount on the right turret side, is to the right; it still carries the lower wading kit assembly fitted before it crossed a beach in Normandy. The M5A1 in the center is equipped with a Culin hedgerow device, another Normandy souvenir. NARA, Signal Corps photo

An M24 issued to the 743d Tank Battalion in February 1945. All four crewmembers are visible. The one to the far left is wearing the insulated winter tanker's helmet and bib-style overalls for warmth. NARA, Signal Corps photo

layout provided room for one hundred forty-seven 37mm shells and 6,500 .30-caliber rounds.

*

By late 1944, the M5A1 light tank was widely viewed as having only limited utility in Europe. Separate battalions in the ETO often drew on Dog Company for medium tank crew replacements. In Italy, light tank crews in the 1st Armored Division were moved to tank dozers, and the light tank companies from two separate tank battalions were seconded to run an armored school.[lii]

Still, a good crew could fight the M5 effectively no matter how mismatched their tank was against German panzers. Consider this extract from the Silver Star citation for S/Sgt. Kenneth Booze, 751st Tank Battalion: "[On 31 January 1944 near Conca, Italy,] Booze, commanding a light tank, engaged a formation of bigger, more heavily armed and armored German Mark IV tanks with such audacious courage and skillful maneuvering that he drove them off and stopped their attempted counterattack. With utter disregard for his own safety, S/Sgt. Booze made a dismounted reconnaissance under heavy

The new M24 and the M5 that it replaced, both of the 744th Tank Battalion (Light). The M24 had slightly thinner armor, similar speed, and a much more powerful main gun. NARA, Signal Corps photo, records of the 744th Tank Battalion

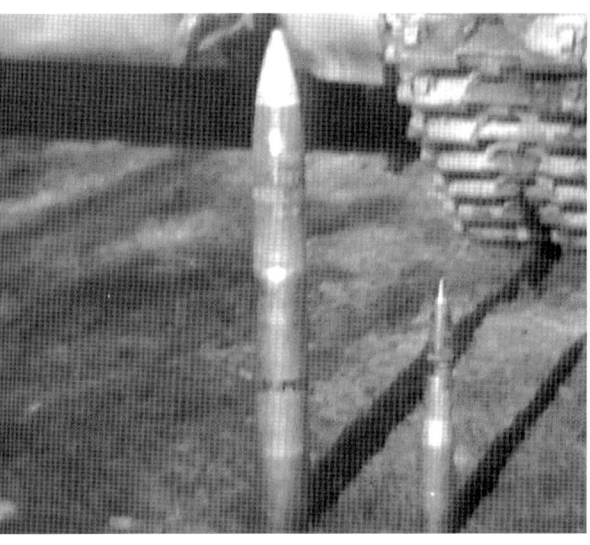

An M24 fires its 75mm main gun, which was as effective as that mounted in the M4 medium tank. Commanders differed after the war as to whether the light tank was worth having even with the improved cannon. NARA, Signal Corps film

A comparison of the Chaffee's 75mm round with the smaller 37mm fired by the M5 series light tanks illustrates why tankers preferred the newer model. NARA, Signal Corps photo

fire of artillery to spot the enemy tanks, then exposed his own light tank to the fire of artillery and three enemy tanks in order to destroy one German Mark IV, thereby forcing the others to withdraw. By skillfully maneuvering his lighter vehicle by coming out of the cover of a house

to fire and then backing quickly under cover again, S/Sgt. Booze avoided getting his own vehicle hit."

The 2d Armored Division's CCB exploited the light tank's speed when one of its battalions lost nearly two-thirds of its medium tanks in futile attacks against

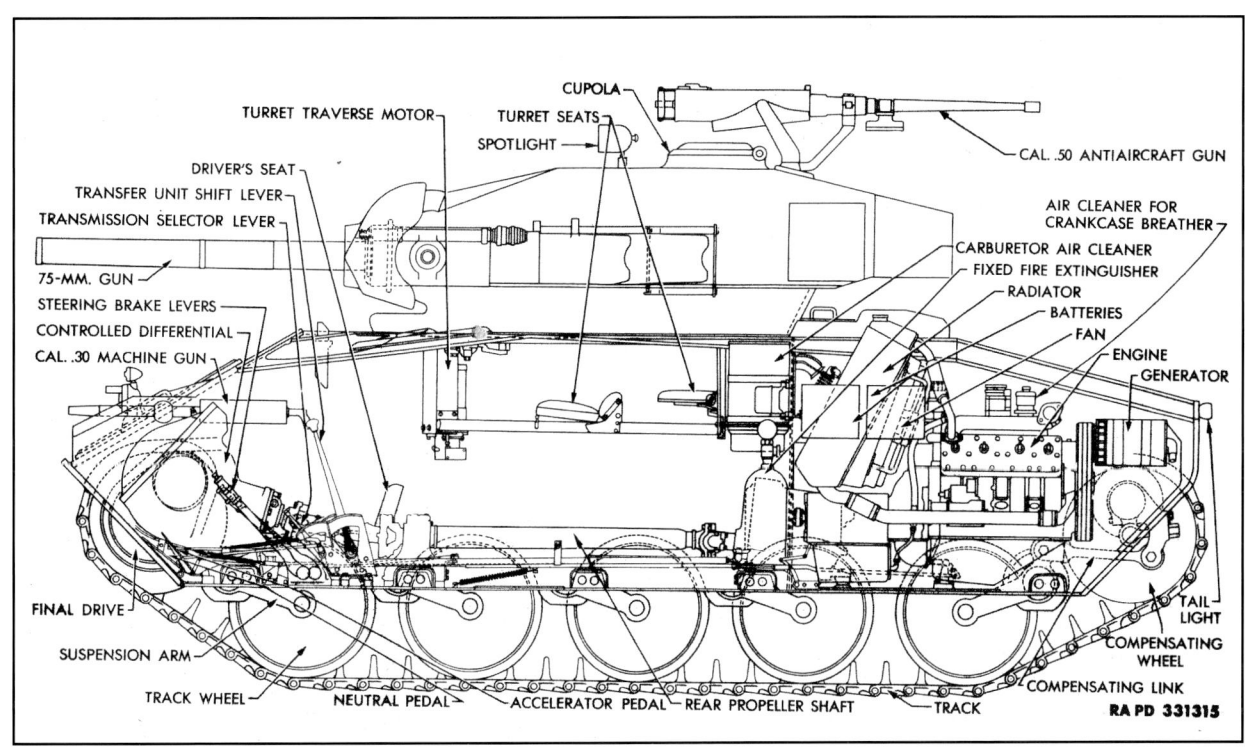

The layout of the M24 Chaffee. NARA, records of the Government Printing Office

The 740th Tank Battalion fielded two M24s after it equipped itself from a repair depot during the Battle of the Bulge and thereby became the first unit to use the Chaffee in battle. Here, one of those M24s supports the 82d Airborne Division in January 1945. Note the collapsible driver's windshield, which most tank models had for use on road marches, and the front hull hatch, which allowed easy access to the transmission. NARA, Signal Corps photo

German positions north of Aachen in October 1944. Lieutenant Colonel E. A. Trahan described the action:

The light tanks burst through the lines of the mediums at 11 AM on the morning of the 6th, throttles wide open and the prayer of every man in the line riding with them. At 35 miles per hour, the M5s screamed toward the enemy in a single weaving line. The German gunners must have thought them mad. Then, as the realization dawned that they could not track these fleeting targets in their sights, the seeds of panic were sowed. The tankers and infantry who were to follow watched in wonder. One thousand yards, and not a tank hit. The mud and soft ground that had made the mediums sitting ducks for the German guns were no great hindrance to the lighter M5s. Two thousand yards, and still not a gap appeared in the charging line. The Germans were firing every weapon they had, and the line was alive with stabbing flashes, but the light tanks seemed to bear charmed lives. Individual Germans began to run to the rear. But every gun in the swiftly

advancing line was firing, and they were cut down before they fairly started. . . .

On the objective, the left of Company [D] overran a strongpoint of artillery and dug-in infantry. The right of the company overran a strongpoint of dug-in antitank guns and infantry at the same time. So rapid had the advance been that the positions were still manned.[liii]

M24 CHAFFEE

The North Africa fighting was still under way when the Army concluded it needed a light tank with the punch of a 75mm gun and improved mobility, and Ordnance authorized development of the new model in March 1943. The M24 Chaffee—the Americans finally took charge of nicknaming their own tanks—was standardized in July 1944 and was the most powerful light tank in the world. Tankers referred to the M24 as the "Panther Pup" because its suspension system and sloped front armor somewhat resembled that of the much larger Panther.

The M24 represented a design break from the M3/M5 light tank series and was closer kin to the M18 tank destroyer and M26 heavy tank. The low-silhouette hull was supported by a torsion-bar suspension. The sleek new turret housed the commander and gunner while the driver and bow gunner remained seated in the hull. The turret had power traverse, but the tank lacked a "little Joe" auxiliary generator, and crews found the powered traverse system rapidly drained the batteries when the engine was not running. The commander's hatch had a vision cupola, and periscopes were provided for the other three crewmen. There was an escape hatch in the floor.

The lightweight, gyrostabilized, short-recoil gun was based on a 75mm design built for use by ground-attack bombers, but it fired the same ammunition at the same muzzle velocity as the weapon mounted in the M4 medium tank. A .30-caliber coaxial machine was supplied, as was a .30-caliber bow gun and a .50-caliber AA machine gun mounted on a prominent pintle on the turret roof. A 2-inch mortar was incorporated into the turret top. Organized stowage was provided for forty-eight 75mm; 3,750 .30-caliber; and four hundred forty .50-caliber rounds, plus fourteen smoke and fragmentation mortar shells. The crew was equipped with four .45-caliber submachine guns or three of those plus an M1 carbine with grenade launcher.

One inch of sloped frontal armor provided the ballistic protection of 2-1/2 inches, while armor on the sides and rear were 1 inch and 3/4 inch thick, respectively.

To simplify production, the twin Cadillac engines were retained from the M5, but with an improved manual shift transfer unit to manage the two Hydra-Matic transmissions. The vehicle weighed in at nearly 20 tons but could reach a top speed of 35 miles per hour on level ground. The tank had a fuel capacity of 110 gallons and a cruising range of 175 miles. The suspension supported a 16-inch-wide track, which was more than 4 inches wider than that on the M5. This better distributed the weight and improved mobility.

The M24 was issued on a much more restricted basis than its predecessors because of lags in delivery, and it served with only a minority of tank battalions, all in Europe. The last four armored divisions to arrive in the ETO had their light tank companies completely outfitted with the new vehicle, reflecting its place as the new standard.

*

Major General Isaac D. White, commanding the 2d Armored Division, on 20 March 1945 wrote to General

A 743d Tank Battalion Chaffee works under fire with 30th Infantry Division doughs near Dorsten on 25 March 1945, shortly after crossing the Rhine River. NARA, Signal Corps photo

Dwight Eisenhower after consulting with his troops on a range of equipment issues, "The M5 light tank should be replaced with the M24 light tank as soon as possible. The latter is a highly satisfactory tank in every respect. [Nonetheless,] every effort should be made to improve the gun, sights, and ammunition."[liv]

No light tank crew willingly sought out German armor, but the M24 could fend for itself if it had to on nearly the same terms as the early Sherman. It had the same fire power, and the disadvantage in armor thickness was all but irrelevant if a high-velocity German gun hit the vehicle. One section of M24s from Company D, 736th Tank Battalion, and an assault gun were working with the 83d Infantry Division near Bockweise, Germany, the evening of 11 April 1945, as recorded in the battalion's AAR: "Immediately east of town at the road junction, the second section encountered an enemy column of two Tiger tanks and several halftracks. Totally unexpected, the enemy came into our position far enough to block the firing of one light tank. The second light tank and one assault gun, however, brought fire on the enemy column, destroying four halftracks, one command car, and one heavy enemy tank. During the fight, our loss was one light tank but no casualties to personnel."

Medium Tanks

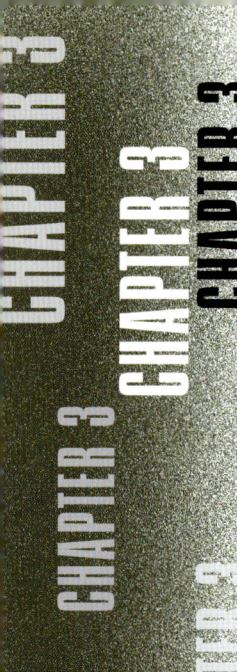

The United States produced a mere fifteen medium tanks the year World War II began, and those were but up-sized versions of the light tanks of the day. Nevertheless, the M2 medium tank of 1939 provided the basis for subsequent models that the tank battalions would fight to victory in 1945, including the M4 Sherman that formed the backbone of the American, British, and Commonwealth armored forces.

The Army had experimented with the Christie suspension system for its medium tanks in the 1930s but selected for mass production a design that would maximize parts commonality with the light tanks it expected to build in even greater numbers. The M2A1 inherited by the Armored Force as its cutting-edge medium tank in 1940 had frontal armor only 1-1/4 inches thick and was armed with a 37mm main gun. Designed as an infantry-support

Above: **An M2A1 medium tank belonging to the 67th Infantry Regiment (Tanks) in 1940. The M2A1 had slightly thicker armor than the M2 and a supercharger on the engine to boost horsepower. Note the two fixed machine guns in the lower glacis armor. The vehicle passed on its chassis, the suspension arrangement, the power train, and much of its superstructure design to the M3.** NARA, Signal Corps photo

Left: **One of the first M3 medium tanks undergoes testing at Aberdeen Proving Ground in April 1941. Note the holes for fixed machine guns beside the left headlamp, the short-barreled 75mm Gun M2 without gyrostabilizer, and the absence of stowage bins on the back deck that were added to later vehicles.** NARA, Signal Corps photo

tank, the M2A1 sprouted machine guns everywhere—two fixed in the hull facing forward, four in sponsons in each corner of the superstructure, and two on the outside of the turret. All these weapons required a six-man crew.

The M2A1 employed the vertical volute spring suspension used on the light tanks but had an extra set of bogies to handle the longer track and greater weight. A nine-cylinder 400 horsepower Wright radial aircraft engine powered the tank, which forced the design of a tall hull to fit the 45-inch wide motor on its side, a constraint that affected all subsequent medium tank designs. (The Wright engine is often singled out for criticism on this score, but all American engines used in medium and heavy tanks during the war required roughly the same amount of vertical space in the engine compartment.) The Armored Force realized the vehicle was already obsolete and only a month after its organization told Ordnance that it needed a medium tank with thicker armor and mounting a 75mm gun.

M3 LEE

The fledgling American tank industry—a community of automobile and locomotive manufacturers that took over production from the small-scale operation at Rock Island Arsenal—initially lacked the capacity to cast a turret large enough to house a 75mm gun, so Ordnance hurriedly designed a stop-gap model. The result was the M3 medium tank, dubbed the Lee by the British after Confederate

Communications

Effective communication among tanks was as important to success in battle as guns, armor, or engines. The Armored Force initially trained crews to respond to hand signals and flags, means that would often prove impractical on the highly lethal modern battlefield. The Army nonetheless realized the importance of radio communications and even before the war installed a receiver in each tank. Yet as late as the Sicilian campaign, not all tanks had two-way radios, which proved a problem in combat when a crew with critical information had no way to pass it on when under fire.

The SCR-245 was the chief tank radio when the Armored Force was born, but development work began in 1940 on the SCR-508 FM family of radios, which became the workhorse in armored battalions.[iv] The line-of-sight SCR-508 system reached out to about 10 miles when a tank was moving and 15 miles when it was sitting still (mechanical operations created interference despite shielding), and in broken terrain tank battalions at times had to use radio-equipped halftracks as relay stations. The SCR-508 had a transmitter and two receivers, while the variant SCR-528 had a transmitter and one receiver, and the SCR-538 had a receiver only. Command tanks were outfitted with the SCR-506 AM radio, which could reach up to 100 miles and tie into other radio nets, such as artillery.

The radio in light tanks was installed in a sponson until the introduction of the M5A1, which had a rear bulge in the turret to house the radio. The FM radio normally went into the left sponson, while the AM radio in a command tank went into the right sponson. The M3 medium tank housed its FM radio in the

The FM Radio Set SCR-508 was the gear used most often by the tankers but could not tie into the infantry net. The push buttons selected among pre-set frequencies. NARA, Signal Corps photo

The AM Radio Set SCR-506 transmitter provided longer-range communications than the SCR-508, though AM radios tended to suffer interference from the tank's electrical system if the engine was running. NARA, Signal Corps photo

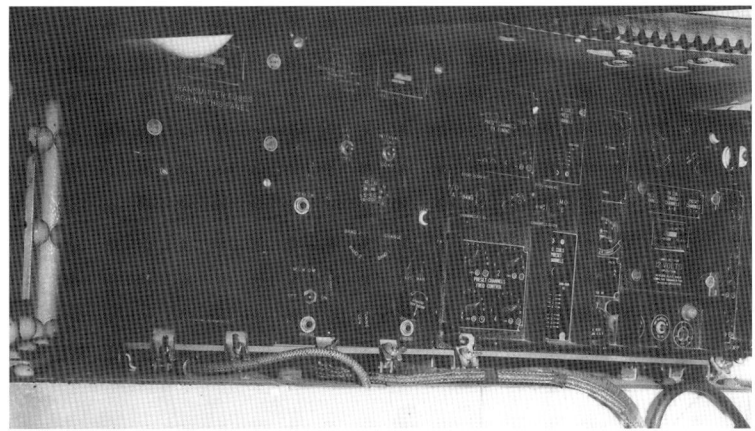

The radio was installed in the sponson of the M3 and early M5 light tanks, in this case an SCR-506 AM command set. The turret gear is visible in the upper right-hand corner. NARA, Signal Corps photo

Principal components of Radio Set SCR-508 installed in the center-rear turret of an M4A3 medium tank. The Tommy gun rack is visible above the radio. The bar in the lower left is the breach guard on the main gun. An intercom box is to the right of the radio set. NARA, Signal Corps photo

turret, although an extra AM radio could be added in the hull of command tanks.

Communications with the infantry were critical for battalions supporting the riflemen. The first workable solution was the installation of a field telephone, generally in a box attached to the rear of the tank. Installation of this field expedient began in separate tank battalions in the ETO in October 1944 and by 1945 the practice was standard in all theaters. In the last year of the war, some tanks were equipped with the AN/VRC3 FM radio, which was a version of the SCR-300 walkie-talkie used by the infantry and which allowed direct communication with the doughs in combat up to a range of about 3 miles.

Few generalizations are possible regarding radio gear in amphibian tank and tractor battalions, as vehicles had to communicate with the Navy, infantry, and regular tank battalions, as well as each other. During one landing, for example, the 708th Provisional Amphibian Tractor Battalion used SCR-508, SCR-510, and Navy TCS-5 radios; the battalion commander subsequently requested SCR-608 and SCR-610 radios in addition. On Okinawa, the same battalion fielded SCR-508, SCR-528, and SCR-300

hull (except in the British model, which had a turret bulge). Subsequent medium tanks carried the radio in the

radios, while the 776th Amphibian Tank Battalion employed SCR-508s and SCR-609s.

A rare picture of an M3 Lee with wading gear; the tank is oriented to the right. This one is crashing through underbrush on Makin Atoll during the first moments of battle on 20 November 1943. NARA, Signal Corps photo

M3 tanks shell the Japanese at King's Wharf, Makin Atoll, on 21 November 1943. These Lees belong to Company A, 193d Tank Battalion. The lower elements of the wading stacks are still mounted. NARA, Signal Corps photo

incorporated a rear bulge for the wireless and eliminated the cupola, and they named this adaptation after Union General Ulysses S. Grant.

The M3 was declared substitute standard in October 1941, but the tank initially served as the backbone of the 1st Armored Division's medium tank battalions in North Africa because of a shortage of M4 tanks. The M3 also soldiered on in the Pacific, where it outclassed all Japanese tank models, until late 1943. It was finally declared obsolete in April 1944.

*

To a young tank force used to puny light tanks and mediums not much larger, the M3 Lee at first looked tremendous. "We drew our first M3s," recalled the informal history of the 741st Tank Battalion, "and we were really proud of them. They appeared invincible. . . ."[lv] The 3d Armored Division's history recorded, "To early tankers. . . General Lee and General Grant battlewagons represented the last word in armored might. It was unthinkable to these men that Germany, winding up a whirlwind campaign in France and the low countries, actually possessed more advanced machines for the waging of total war. This, however, was the case."[lvi]

The first American tankers to fight the Germans were from three volunteer crews that joined the British in Libya to gain battle experience in the M3. Major Henry Cabot Lodge Jr., their commander, briefly described their first action near Acoma on 11 June 1941: "[The crews]

swung their tanks beside British-manned tanks and were promptly attacked by German tanks at a range of about 4,000 yards. All day the American crews kept up a withering fire. . . [and] knocked out at least eight German panzers before the Germans brought up their 88mm guns and the British gave the order to retreat."[lvii]

Designers had considered the 37mm gun the primary antitank weapon on the M3, but British battle reports in early 1942 indicated that crews were using the 75mm gun because of its greater range and hitting power. The British found the tank at least equal to the Mark IV and reported that the armor was effective against fire from guns up to 50mm. American crews in North Africa later provided similar feedback but complained about the limited traverse of the main gun.[lviii]

Major General Ernest Harmon, who took command of the 1st Armored Division after the Kasserine debacle, nonetheless opined that the tank was "obsolete by the time we got it on the battlefield."[lix] Colonel Henry Gardiner, who commanded the M3-equipped 2d/13th Armored Regiment in North Africa, deemed the Lee "much inferior" to the Sherman. "The tank could only fire [the 75mm gun] in the direction it was headed. Moreover, the gun was set so low that almost the whole tank had to be exposed before it could be brought to bear on a target. There was no slope to the side armor, and the .30-caliber gun in the cupola, which was for defense against aircraft, was worse than useless."[lx]

M4 SHERMAN

The M4 medium tank, named by the British after Union General William Tecumsah Sherman, was the most important tank in Allied service and did not lag all that far behind the interim M3 Lee. The M4 was standardized in October 1941, little more than a year after the Armored Force had demanded such a tank from Ordnance, and the Sherman remained in production throughout the war, undergoing a large number of modifications in response to battlefield developments.

The T6 medium tank pilot was completed in September 1941, nine months after the first M3 Lee. At that time, it was the cutting edge of tank technology. NARA, Signal Corps photo

EARLY MODELS

The Sherman inherited the chassis, suspension, and power train of the M3, but the gyrostabilized 75mm gun moved to a fully traversing cast turret powered by hydraulic and manual systems. Tank commanders—who had a simple steel sight on the turret top—could override the gunner's control of the turret rotation, but their switch lacked fine calibration, which meant the gunner still had to make final adjustments on the target in most cases. The turret turned quickly, a trait crews came to value highly because it often meant the Sherman got in the first accurate shot against heavier German panzers that had manual traverse systems. The turret included a basket for the crew.

The decision to stick with the 75mm main gun rested on the fact that it fired an excellent HE round—in keeping with the doctrinal assumption that tanks should avoid fighting other tanks—but it nevertheless had plenty of armor-piercing punch for the battlefield of 1941. The main gun fired an APC round at a muzzle velocity of 2,030 feet per second and could penetrate 3.1 inches of face-hardened plate at 1,000 yards, which provided a considerable comfort margin over the 2-inch-thick armor on the front of Germany's then cutting edge Mark IV medium tank. The early combination gun mount M34 incorporated a .30-caliber coaxial machine gun. A

A line of tanks at Fort Knox. An early M4 is closest, followed by an M3 and an M3A1. The sixth tank in line is an M4A1. Light tanks are seen toward the rear of the column. Library of Congress, Prints & Photographs Division, FSA-OWI Collection

An M4, probably from the 2d Armored Division, fires indirectly during the Roer River offensive in November 1944. The 75mm gun produced a modest muzzle blast. NARA, Signal Corps film

View from the commander's hatch of the M4's 75mm main gun firing. The commander had the best view of the battlefield of any man in the tank, and he could override the gunner's control of the turret rotation to move the gun toward a target he has just spotted. NARA, Signal Corps film

narrow front shield protected only the 75mm gun, while the machine gun protruded through a slit in the turret front. In October 1942, Ordnance standardized the M34A1 gun mount, the mantlet of which also protected the machine gun and incorporated a telescopic sight for the main gun.

The cult of massed machine guns finally expired after the first production models, which had two fixed .30-calibers in the glacis as in the M3, and all Shermans used in combat had only a second .30-caliber positioned in a ball mount in the glacis at the assistant driver/bow gunner's position. A .50-caliber machine gun for AA defense was normally mounted on a ring around the

commander's split-hatch in the turret. A 2-inch smoke mortar in the turret roof was standard equipment, although it seems rarely to have been used in action.

The M4A1, which had a cast hull, preceded the welded-hull M4 into production, but the two were nearly identical in other respects. The 34-ton (combat loaded) vehicle had sloped frontal armor 2 inches thick that provided the ballistic protection of 4 inches. The welded model, however, had forward-jutting hatch areas for the driver and bow gunner, the vertical faces of which offered less protection and proved prone to snag enemy rounds in "shot traps." The upper hull sides were 2

The cast-hull M4A1 preceded the welded-hull M4 into production. The first Shermans issued to the Armored Force had two fixed machine guns in the hull front and bogie assemblies with the return rollers above the center. The extra MGs were dropped almost immediately, and the return rollers were soon shifted back and replaced at the top of the bogie assembly by a skid plate. NARA, Signal Corps photo

The M3 and new M4A1 medium tanks in spring 1942. The early M4A1 had solid vision blocks for the driver and bow gunner instead of periscopes. The bulge atop the M4A1 turret is an early version of the main gun sight; the gun itself is missing. NARA, Signal Corps photo

The turret basket of an M4 tank from the 34th Armored Regiment, 5th Armored Division. Trouble occasionally arose in battle if the gun crew needed ammunition passed up from the hull, but the turret was rotated so that the mesh was in the way. NARA, Signal Corps photo

M4A1s from the 760th Tank Battalion near Turo, Italy, on 12 May 1944. The original hatches for the driver and bow gunner were an extremely tight fit. The lead tank has appliqué armor over the gunner's position. NARA, Signal Corps photo

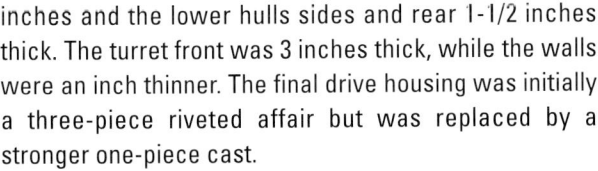

An unfortunate incident involving a bomb crater near Littoria, Italy, provides a top view of an M4A1. All three members of the turret crew had to make it out of the single hatch in case the tank caught fire. Periscopes are visible in the driver's and commander's hatches. NARA, Signal Corps photo

The composite hull, which mated a cast glacis with a welded main hull, was produced in limited numbers during the late production cycle of the M4 with the 75mm gun. NARA, Signal Corps photo

inches and the lower hulls sides and rear 1-1/2 inches thick. The turret front was 3 inches thick, while the walls were an inch thinner. The final drive housing was initially a three-piece riveted affair but was replaced by a stronger one-piece cast.

The M4A1 had organized stowage for ninety 75mm shells, and the slab-sided M4 for ninety-seven, typically a mix of HE, AP, and white phosphorous (WP). (Actual aggregate expenditures of tank and TD 75mm, 76mm, and 90mm ammunition in the ETO were roughly 70 percent HE, 20 percent AP, and 10 percent WP.)[lxi] Both models

provided space for 4,750 .30-caliber and three hundred .50-caliber rounds.

Ordnance in 1943 introduced a new 47-degree glacis on the welded-hull models to correct the shot trap caused by protruding hatches. The new glacis design reduced the slope from 56 degrees, and in order to compensate for the reduced ballistic protection, the front armor was increased to 2-1/2 inches. By D-Day in June 1944, the Army also had added one-inch-thick armored plate to provide more protection to the sponson ammo racks and welded angled armor pieces in front of the old hatches on fielded Shermans with the 56-degree glacis.

An M4 with the 56-degree glacis operates with the Americal Division on Bougainville in February 1944. This tank has appliqué armor in front of the hull hatches and over the sponson ammo racks (one on the left side and two on the right). It also has extra armor around the lower part of the turret, a modification most often seen in the Pacific Theater. NARA, Signal Corps photo

A venerable 712th Tank Battalion M4 advances with riflemen near St, Jores, France, on 7 July 1944. The tank displays the elimination of the hatch shot traps accomplished by welding angled iron plates in front of them. It also has appliqué armor on the right turret side over the gunner's position. NARA, Signal Corps photo

Many tanks also received appliqué armor on the turret side at the gunner's position by that time. During the fighting in late 1944, the Army produced one-inch armor kits to be welded onto the 47-degree glacis, although ordnance shops in the field managed to mount them on all hull variants.

The Sherman earned an unenviable reputation for catching fire after being penetrated by enemy rounds, and as early as the North Africa fighting, the Armored Force found that a majority of wounds incurred in its ranks were burns. Tankers believed that the gasoline engines were the cause of the blazes, but studies revealed that the culprit was propellant from the Sherman's own ammo. In response, the Army in 1943

This 105mm Sherman assault gun clearly displays the 47-degree glacis, which both eliminated the shot traps and provided bigger hatches to the driver and bog. NARA, Signal Corps photo

An M4A3E8 with a 1-inch add-on armor plate kit welded to the glacis. The loader's position is fitted out with an old-style commanders ring hatch. NARA, Signal Corps photo

Tankers resorted to field expedients to reduce the likelihood of a penetration, at least by the ubiquitous German bazooka-style weapons. They first turned to sandbags during the fighting in Normandy; tests offered mixed results as to whether the bags worked, but they made tankers feel safer. Here, a 3d Armored Division Sherman displays a typical sandbagging job near Stolberg, Germany, on 14 October 1944. NARA, Signal Corps film

A 2d Armored Division M4A3 (76mm) displays another field expedient armor: a layer of concrete poured on the glacis. Experiments conducted by the 709th Tank Battalion in February 1945 indicated that poured concrete did not stop bazookas from penetrating the armor plate, but that it did reduce the splash of molten steel inside the tank caused by the warhead to "negligible" proportions. NARA, Signal Corps photo

introduced ammunition stowage racks surrounded by water, but the new arrangement did not reach troops until 1944. "Wet stowage," moreover, did not eliminate the problem because crews tended to carry extra ammunition into battle stacked on the tank floor.

Industry could not meet demand for a single engine type as Sherman production took off, so several power plants came into use. The Whirlwind radial engine carried over from the M3 could move the Sherman at speeds up to 24 miles per hour on level ground. The fuel capacity was 175 gallons, which provided a cruising range of 120 miles. The M4A3, standardized in January 1942, had a welded hull and was equipped with a 500-horsepower V-8 Ford engine that increased the maximum speed to 26 miles per hour. This engine variant became the favorite in Army tank units because it was easier to maintain and provided greater horsepower, although it served in smaller numbers than did the Wright Whirlwind. The M4A2, equipped with twin diesel engines supplying a combined 375 horsepower, was standardized in December 1941. Only some thirty-three copies of this model appear to have served in combat with Army tank battalions, specifically with the 1st Armored Division in North Africa, but it was the variant of choice in the Marine Corps because it shared fuel type with Navy landing craft.[lxii]

The five-man crew included commander, gunner, loader, driver, and assistant driver/bow gunner. The tank had an intercom and was equipped with the SCR-508 FM radio (plus SCR-506 AM radio in command tanks). All crewmen had periscopes, and the gunner's incorporated his telescopic sight in tanks equipped with the M34 combination gun mount. Early models had direct-vision blocks with thick glass and armored covers for the driver and bow gunner, which were soon replaced by a fixed periscope in front of the hatches, which had rotating periscopes. An escape hatch was added in the floor after

The Ford V-8 engine became the preferred type in the Sherman and also powered the M26 Pershing. The engine did not suffer clogged plugs like the radial engine when run at low rpm.
NARA, records of the Chief of Ordinance

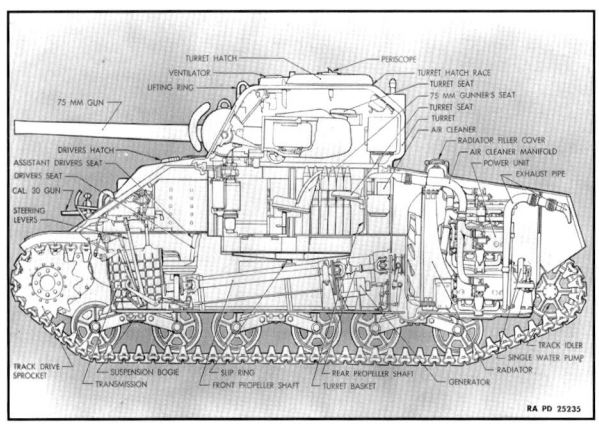

This diagram of the M4A4, which was used for training by some American battalions but was mainly supplied to the Allies under Lend-Lease, shows a typical internal Sherman layout. The M4A4 had five automobile engines welded together and a slightly longer hull to fit them. NARA, records of the Chief of Ordinance

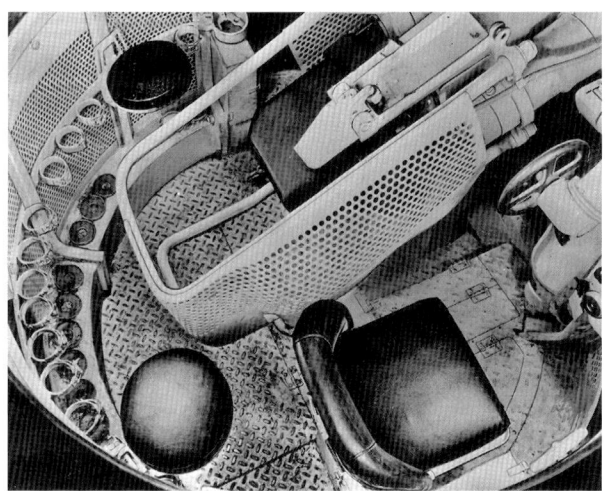

View of the turret interior in a 75mm Sherman. The seats, clockwise from the upper one, are the loader's, the gunner's and the commander's. The hoops on the turret basket are the ammunition ready racks. NARA, records of the Chief of Ordnance

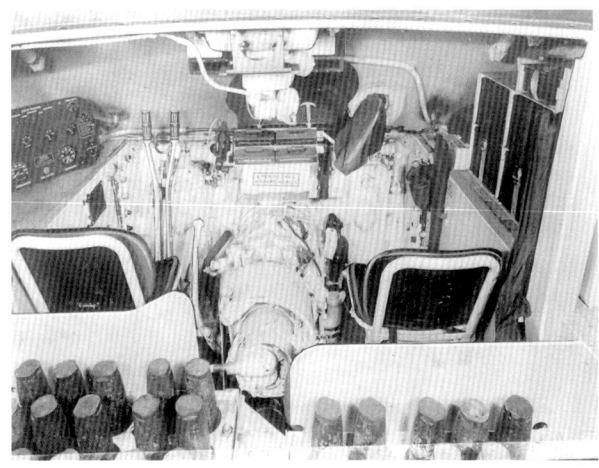

Interior of the M4 hull; the bow machine gun is covered. The transmission is between the two seats, and the driver's steering levers, which applied the brakes to the two tracks, are visible. Note the ammunition racks behind the seats; one of the bog's jobs was to pass shells up into the turret basket. NARA, records of the Chief of Ordnance

Lee-style side access doors were dropped from the pilot T6 model. Crews were issued one .45-caliber submachine gun, four pistols, and twelve assorted hand grenades.

Driving the Sherman demanded a great deal of work. The five-speed transmission required double-clutching, and the driver steered the tank by pulling hard on levers that braked the left or right track.

*

American tankers were assured by the Army that they had the finest tank in the world, and in January 1943,

Lt. Col. E. A. Russell, executive officer of CCB, 1st Armored Division, then fighting in Tunisia, agreed, telling an Army observer, "The M4 tank is the best tank in the theater." Lieutenant Colonel Louis Hightower, who led the 2/1st Armored Regiment counterattack at Sidi bou Zid the first day of the Kasserine Pass battle, reported a second engagement hours later that showed the Sherman could indeed fight:

Suddenly we heard gunfire, and coming over a rise we came upon a debacle.

This almost certainly is part of Lt. Col. Louis Hightower's 2d Battalion retreating toward Sbeitla on 14 February 1943. An M4A1, recognizable by its smoothly curving cast hull, pulls a halftrack across a dry riverbed near Sidi bou Zid. NARA, Signal Corps photo

A German Mark IV knocked out by artillery fire at Kasserine Pass only days after Hightower's shootout. With the long 75mm gun, the panzer was a rough match for the Sherman. NARA, Signal Corps photo

Nine Mark IVs and a Tiger were shooting up one of our columns of halftracks and light vehicles. The gun on the other medium tank [in headquarters section] was jammed, and the two light tanks were too thinly armored for the task before us, [so] I sent them away. I ordered our column of light vehicles to swing in behind us, as my driver raced to put us between them and the Germans.

As the Germans turned for what they thought would be a picnic, we let go and struck their commander's tanks with our third shot. He stopped cold as if he had hit a tree. We got a second tank with one more shot, and the German tanks braked to a halt and began to fire at us in earnest. We could fire on the move, though, and kept going at about 15 mile per hour. We put three more shots into another German tank before discovering that it was the Tiger. I saw the shells burst against him, but I don't know if he was disabled. However, he didn't shoot at us again, so we must have done some damage.

Another Mark IV came up to him, and we got that one with one shot, still moving ourselves. He flamed up like a flower. Another Mark IV approached the Tiger and the burning tank, which was stupid because all my gunner had to do was move his sight over a hair, and that tank also flamed up with the first shot. Then our gun overheated and jammed, and we were in serious trouble as the remaining Mark IVs really opened up on us. We could actually see the shells coming along close to the ground, like a ricocheting stone on the water. One shell fragment came straight down our gun tube and rattled around the turret but caused no serious damage.

Another shell went through the bogie wheels, under the tank. Then with a sound like a giant bell, a shell hit our turret, but didn't penetrate. Another hit made our ears ring, but we kept on working on that jammed breech-block. As soon as our gun was unjammed, we began firing again, but now a German 75mm shell smashed the bottom of our left gas tank, and blazing gasoline spurted out over the back of the tank, the tracks, and the ground around us. Heavy black smoke began to roll up from our hull. I shouted to my boys, "Now is the time to git," and we boiled out like peas from a hot pod. . . .[lxiii]

The few early encounters with Tigers in North Africa and Sicily and then run-ins with Mark V Panther tanks beginning in early 1944 nevertheless gradually convinced tankers they had problems. All tanks common in German service after North Africa could penetrate the thickest armor of the Sherman at all ordinary combat ranges and had superior optics that allowed accurate gunnery at longer distances. Indeed, the literature is rife with tales of rounds from the Panther's long-barreled, high-velocity 75mm cannon and the Tiger's powerful 88mm gun penetrating Shermans and exiting the other side of the tank. The Sherman's 75mm gun, meanwhile, could deal effectively with the widely used Mark IV but it could not penetrate the glacis of the Panther or Tiger from any range.

Lieutenant Homer Wilkes from the 747th Tank Battalion described an encounter between his platoon and a Tiger on 20 November 1944:

A 747th Tank Battalion Sherman on the Roer plain two days before Sgt. Herman Deaver's encounter with a Tiger in one of this vehicle's sisters. This tank is in close proximity to the enemy, and the commander, whose head is out of his hatch, is using the covers to protect himself from snipers. NARA, Signal Corps photo

An M26 fires at German positions on the far side of the Rhine River in March 1945. Only a handful of the new model saw action with the Armored Force before the end of the war. NARA, Signal Corps photo

and also disliked the layout of ammunition stowage.[lxvii] The Pershing, moreover, could carry only seventy rounds of the 90mm ammo. Nonetheless, the Americans had bought into the Soviet-German arms race for ever bigger guns and ever thicker armor on tanks.

The M26 had the usual layout of a .30-caliber machine each in the coaxial and bow gun positions, plus a .50-caliber machine gun for antiaircraft defense. The same Ford V-8 used in the M4A3 powered the tank. Due to its much greater weight, the M26 could reach a maximum speed of only 20 miles per hour, and it was prone to mechanical problems because it was underpowered.

*

The Pershing proved it was a rough match for German heavy tanks, which is to say it could both kill and be killed. Sergeant Nick Mashlonik commanded a 3d Armored Division T26E3 at Elsdorf, Germany, where 2/33d Armored Regiment tangled with the 9th Panzer Division on 26-27 February. A Tiger knocked out one Pershing; later, Mashlonik told military historian George Forty:

A 3d Armored Division M26 in action during street fighting in Cologne in early March 1945. This Pershing engaged and destroyed a Mark V Panther in the main square. NARA, Signal Corps film

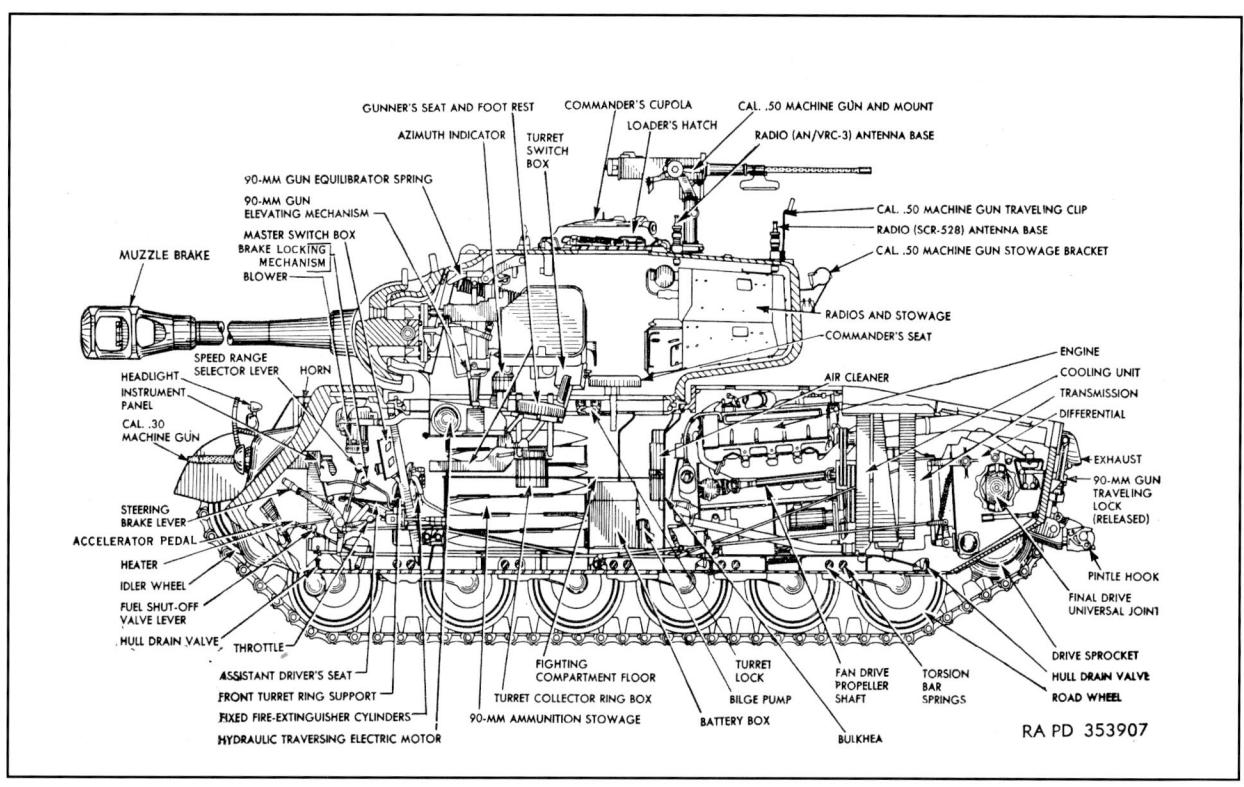

Internal layout of the M26 Pershing. NARA, records of the Government Printing Office

Our casualties kept mounting, and the CO of our company asked me if I though I could knock out the Tiger that was almost destroying us.... The Tiger was slightly dug in, and this meant it would be more difficult to destroy....

Just as we started our tank and had moved very slowly forward (creeping) I noticed that the Tiger was moving out of position and exposing his belly to us. I immediately put a shot in its belly and knocked it off. The second shot was fired at his track and knocked the right-hand track off. The third shot was fired at the turret, and the HE point-detonating destroyed the escaping crew.

At that time, three other German armored vehicles were leaving Elsdorf and were on the road to my right flank. I waited until all of them were on the road with their rear ends exposed and then I picked off each one with one shell each, getting the last one first, then the second one, and then the first one—just like shooting ducks. Then I came back to each vehicle with HE point-detonating and destroyed the crews as they were dismounting from the burning vehicles.[lxviii]

Amphibious Tanks

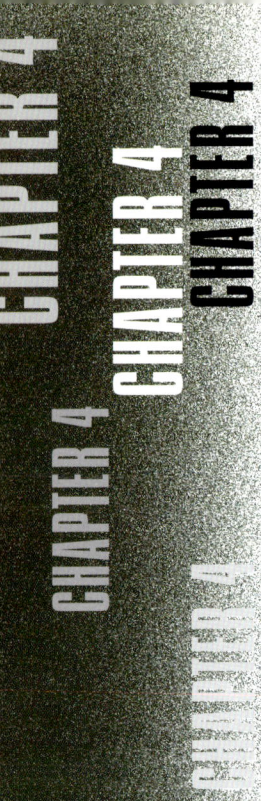

Reaching the enemy in every theater required an amphibious assault at some point. Unlike in the movies, landing craft did not hit the beach, drop their ramps, and disgorge masses of tanks in the first wave. Instead, amphibious armored vehicles emerged as the best way to give assaulting infantry close-in fire support on hostile shores. "Amphibians" were truly at home in the water as one land, while the duplex drive tank "amphibious" tank had just enough sea worthiness to get from ship to shore under benign sea conditions.

AMTRACS

Amphibian tractor battalions used tracked vehicles that, despite the tractor name, carried people rather than towing things. Amtrac troop carriers proved a necessity for storming many islands the Pacific, where reefs around atolls often prevented landing craft from reaching a beach at all, and they provided fire support once on shore.

Above: **LVT(1)s, these belonging to the Marine Corps, head for the beach at Guadalcanal in August 1942. The amtracs only carried cargo during this, their first appearance.**
U.S. Navy photo

Left: **An LVT(2) and three-man crew. The two Japanese flags painted under the vehicle's nickname suggest the crew has downed two enemy planes with the on-board machine guns.**
NARA, 708th Amphibian Tank Battalion records

The amtrac was first developed for rescue work in the Everglades and was initially adapted to military use by the U.S. Marine Corps. The nomenclature was changed to landing vehicle, tracked (LVT), to match the Navy's designation for landing craft, but the "amtrac" shorthand remained in general use. Amtracs were of light steel construction and often carried add-on armor for assaults; were equipped with machine guns to support the infantry; and in some ways came to resemble the light tank of the pre-war period in actual use once ashore.

The first military model, the T33/LVT(1) Alligator, was unarmored and of sheet metal construction. The cargo area had room for twenty-four men with packs and rifles or 4,500 pounds of cargo. Gun rails ran around the sides and rear, and the vehicle usually had one .30-caliber and one .50-caliber machine gun mounted to the sides. A six-cylinder Hercules WLXC3 gasoline engine powered the LVT(1), and tracks that used blocks with scoop-shaped blades provided the motive force in the water as well as on land.

The LVT(2), LVT(A)(2), and LVT(4) Water Buffalos descended directly from the Alligator and outfitted the Army's amtrac battalions. The LVT(2) was still constructed of sheet steel while the LVT(A)(2) was made of armor plate, which increased the weight slightly from 30,900 pounds to 16 tons. Both vehicles had gun rails forward and to the sides and rear, which allowed machine guns to be mounted to fire in any direction, and twin forward-facing machine guns protected by shields became a common configuration. Thirty fully equipped infantrymen could be ferried to the beach, and they had

The LVT(1) Alligator did not serve in battle with the Army, but even official sources sometimes referred to later models by that name. The side pontoons on the LVT(1) were taller and covered more of the suspension system than on models used by Army battalions.
NARA, Signal Corps photo

to exit by clambering over the sides, often under fire. The LVT(4)—the most common model in Army use—closely resembled the LVT(2) but had an armored cab and an armored rear ramp that could be lowered with a hand crank to allow the vehicle to carry a jeep, small anti-tank gun, or field piece and enabled riflemen to debark in greater safety. The LVT(4) had two swinging

and two stationary machine-gun mounts.

These models were longer and wider than the Alligator, had an improved and highly flexible suspension system, and used the same seven-cylinder aircraft engine that powered the M3 light tank. The amtrac could reach speeds of about 25 miles per hour on land and 6 miles per hour in the water. It made a stable enough boat, but a large wave or rough surf greater than 5 feet could swamp or overturn one.[lxix]

A crew of three men managed the LVT(2) and LVT(A)(2). The commander/driver, assistant driver, and radio operator sat in the cab. A post-war survey in the Pacific Theater indicated that amtrac units wanted a fourth man added to the LVT crew because the assault infantry manned most of the on-board machine guns during the run to the beach, and once the riflemen left the vehicle the three-man crew could not adequately service the weapons just when that fire power was vitally needed.[lxx]

In the LVT(4), the engine separated the commander and the driver in the front cabin. Field expedients to overcome this problem included "reins" on which the commander could pull to signal the driver and simple mechanical panels resembling a ship's telegraph with commands such as start, stop, left, right, and speed changes. The LVT(4) often had a fourth crewman assigned to operate the rear ramp, which left the problem of manning machine guns unresolved. Although not formally part of the table of organization and equipment, some LVT(4)s were modified to serve as ambulances by installing racks capable of holding six litters.[lxxi]

*

Lieutenant Russell Gugeler interviewed men from the 773d, 715th, and 534th Amphibian Tractor battalions, which provided about half the LVT lift for the Marine assault on Saipan on 15 June 1944, and recorded the 773d's experience in the assault wave: "The enemy mortar and artillery fire, which had been scattered beyond the reef, became intense as the vehicles neared [the beach]. Our own bombardment of the enemy beach had caused a cloud of smoke and dust, which obscured

The LVT(A)(2), top view. The tube down the center of the passenger compartment is the drive (propeller) shaft running from the rear-mounted engine to the final drive forward. NARA, records of the Government Printing Office

An LVT(4) under way during the landings on Angaur in the Pelau Islands on 17 September 1944. The tracks provided the motive force in the water. NARA, Signal Corps film

LVT(4)s approach Manila on 7 February 1945 after a lengthy overland journey. The amphibians provided both direct support and river-crossing capabilities to advancing troops, who had no need to wait for assault boats or bridging equipment. NARA, Signal Corps photo

A view of the LVT(4)'s ramp, troop/cargo space, and machine gun positions. Note the scoops on the track blocks that enabled movement in water and the damage to the right track, possibly caused by hard surfaces on shore. NARA, Signal Corps photo

A Water Buffalo, probably manned by a crew from the 747th Tank Battalion, supports the assault crossing of the Rhine by the 30th Infantry Division on 24 March 1945. NARA, Signal Corps photo

LVT(A)(4) (near left) and LVT(A)(1) (near right) amtanks, almost certainly from the 708th Amphibian Tank Battalion, head for the beach on Okinawa. Extra .30-caliber machine guns mounted at the side hatches of the LVT(A)(4)s are just visible. NARA, Signal Corps photo

any point targets. . . . By the time the [am]tanks had reached the shore, the first tractors had crept up to within 50 yards of them, and the two waves jammed up on the narrow beach. Between the reef and the shore, both Companies A and B lost one tractor from the heavy shellfire. Sergeant James A. McLean, a tractor commander, was just behind [Sgt. Edward] Dombrowski's

demolished tank when his tractor received three direct hits from mortar fire. Thirteen of the twenty-eight men in McLean's vehicle were killed, and only the assistant driver, Pfc. Ralph L. Schlessinger, escaped any injury. The other tractor, which belonged to Sgt. Steven Spradley, was knocked out by small-arms fire and later towed inland. Spradley operated the machine guns until the grips of the gun were shot out of his hands. Private First Class Peter Wilson, another tractor commander, had located the gun that hit Dombrowski's tank and had silenced it with machine gun fire."[lxxii]

The 718th Amphibian Tractor Battalion, which participated in the raids deep behind Japanese lines on Leyte in the Philippines in late 1944 and early 1945, observed, "One of the most noticeable facts of the operations on the west coast was the increased appreciation of the LVT as a combat vehicle both by the crews and by the infantry. It was found that under suitable conditions, LVTs were excellent close-support vehicles. . . . An armor-plated LVT will turn back small-arms, light machine-gun, and grenade fire, and its automatic weapon fire power lends it to both defensive and offensive action. It was also found that LVTs were capable of providing excellent fire protection against low-level air attacks."[lxxiii]

Although the vast majority of amtracs served in the Pacific Theater, the European commands received more than five hundred. One company from the 739th Medium Tank Battalion, Special (Mine Exploder) operated twenty-seven LVTs to ferry infantry across the Roer River in March 1945. The 747th Tank Battalion (later briefly converted to an amphibian tractor battalion) traded in its tanks for amtracs to ferry the infantry across the Rhine in March 1945; each company was issued seventeen LVT(2)s and eight LVT(4)s. The 752d and 755th Tank battalions in Italy similarly employed amtracs for the Po River crossings in April 1945.

AMTANKS

Amphibian tanks were built on the LVT(2) amtrac chassis and were designed to provide the assault wave with tank gun support on the beach. They had the same drive train as the LVT(2) and reached similar top speeds on both land and water but were more stable at sea because of their greater weight and could likewise bull through up to 8 feet of surf.[lxxiv] With armor ranging from 1/4 inch on the flanks to 1/2 inch to the front, they were suitable for general use only in the Pacific Theater, where the threat from Japanese tanks and antitank guns was relatively low.

An LVT(A)(1) amtank and crew. Note the M5 tank turret and, behind that, the right-side scarf mount (facing to rear) for a .30-caliber machine gun. NARA, 708th Amphibian Tank Battalion records

The 16-ton LVT(A)(1) was basically a covered amtrac with an M5 light tank turret mounted on top. As on the M5, the amtank had a 37mm main gun and a .30-caliber coaxial machine gun, and the roomy vehicle carried a hundred four shells for the cannon and six thousand machine-gun rounds. The turret had both hydraulic and manual traverse systems, and twin hatches were provided. The commander had two periscopes and the gunner one that incorporated his sight. Twin hatches on the rear deck had scarf mounts for .30-caliber machine guns. The six-man crew included commander, driver, assistant driver/radio operator, 37mm gunner, and two scarf machine gunners. The vehicle had a radio and intercom system.

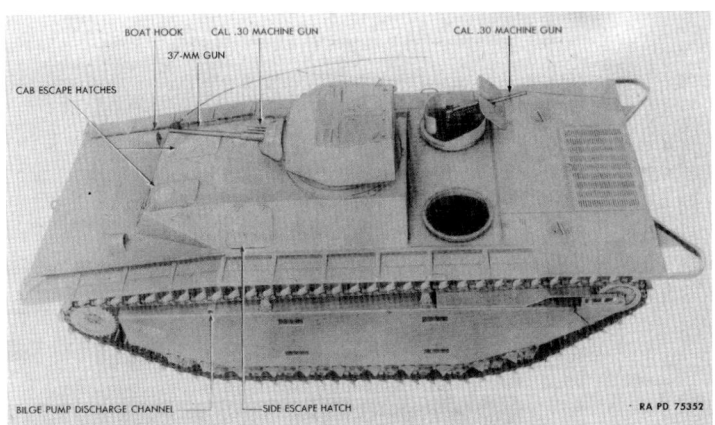

LVT(A)(1), top view. NARA, records of the Government Printing Office

Crews found the 37mm gun powerful enough for coconut tree log bunkers and simple concrete pill-boxes encountered early on but inadequate for many prepared positions as the enemy dug ever deeper into the islands. The gun could handle Japanese tanks, but such encounters were rare. The scarf guns turned out to be the most important weapons on the tank. After landing, gunners fired into trees to eliminate snipers, and many times they saved their vehicles during close Japanese infantry assaults. On the other hand, scarf gunners suffered the highest casualty rate because they had little protection.

LVT(A)(1)s on Okinawa work with the 96th Infantry Division on 1 April 1945. The right scarf gunner's helmet on the nearest amtank is just visible above the lip of his armored shield. NARA, Signal Corps photo

The LVT(A)(4) was similar in design to the LVT(A)(1) but carried the turret from the M8 Howitzer Motor Carriage assault gun mounted further toward the stern for proper trim (which eliminated the scarf gun positions) and weighed nearly 17 tons. The open-topped turret had a short-barreled 75mm howitzer and a .50-caliber machine gun mounted to the rear, and the vehicle carried a hundred rounds for the main gun and four hundred for the machine gun. The vehicle had a crew of six men, including commander, driver, assistant driver-radio operator, gunner, assistant gunner, and ammunition handler. The vehicle had a radio and intercom system.

Crews liked the new gun but found the amtank vulnerable to Japanese infantry attacks as the commander had to fully expose himself to fire the .50-caliber machine gun at a ground target. LVT(A)(4) and LVT(A)(1) amtanks were intermingled in platoons so that the latter could provide close-in covering fire, and a .30-caliber hull machine gun fired by the assistant driver was added to late-production LVT(A)(4)s. Some units mounted extra .30-caliber machine guns into the two side hatches.

Another field modification was add-on armor plate to better protect the engine and pontoons.

LVT(A)(4)s began reaching units in May 1944 and first served with the 708th Amphibian Tank Battalion during the invasion of Saipan on 15 June. With the addition of the 75mm howitzer, one experienced commander assessed that an amtank battalion could give a good account of itself against even one or two Japanese destroyers should it be intercepted during a water march close to shore.

In light of the vulnerability of amtanks as compared with land tanks, Central Pacific Base Command and Tenth Army subsequently established a guide for the use of LVT(A)(4)s as artillery after initial landings. Artillery missions became an important secondary function of the howitzer-armed amtanks; amtanks nonetheless again provided close support to infantry advancing inland during subsequent landings in the Philippine and Ryukyu islands, including Okinawa.[lxxv]

*

Amphibians started into battle by leaving an LST, and, commented one report, "the difficulty of such move-

An LVT(A)(4) and crew. This vehicle does not have the .50-caliber turret antiaircraft machine gun mounted—the only weapon initially available for use against attacking infantry. NARA, 708th Amphibian Tank Battalion records

An LVT(A)(4) on Hokaji Shima, Ryukyu Islands, on 26 March 1945 reveals its open-topped turret, nearly identical to the one on the M8 assault gun. The amtank has a bow machine gun and sandbags for extra protection, and the main gun is elevated to fire indirectly. NARA, Signal Corps photo

ment can be fully appreciated only by an eyewitness. The LST is not a readily maneuverable vessel, and it is peculiarly subject to rolling and pitching. The heavy amphibian tank must be driven off the ramp without damaging ship or tank. Its return is even more complicated."[lxxvi] The fact that the driver could not quickly stop an amphibian in the water—the scoops on the tracks faced only one way, so reversing thrust only slowed the ungainly vessels slightly—helps explain why[lxxvii]

Captain John Straub, who commanded the LVTs of Dog Group, 708th Provisional Amphibian Tractor Battalion, described the Army's first armored amphibian landing at Kwajalein on 31 January

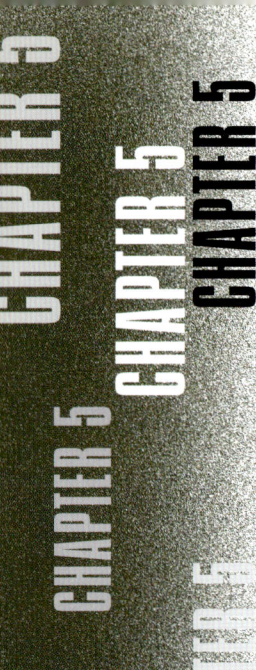

Specials and Variants

The ubiquitous Sherman served as the basis for many variants created to make the tank battalions even more lethal in battle. The U.S. Army nonetheless never jumped into the design of custom "funnies" with the same wild enthusiasm as the British, who fielded an entire division—the 79th Armored—equipped with a menagerie of specialized tanks.

TANK DOZER

Of the various specials, the unheralded tank dozer probably made the greatest contribution in battle. A standard bulldozer blade was attached to a Sherman and pivoted on brackets incorporated into the middle bogie assemblies of the tank. A hydraulic jack, mounted on the outside front of the tank and powered by an oil pump driven off the drive shaft, raised and lowered the blade. The driver could jettison the gear in just ten seconds, and the tank could fight with the blade still on. The only real drawback to the design was that the extra 7,000 pounds

Above: **A tank dozer in Normandy in July 1944, where the remarkably flexible vehicle was in the thick of the action from the assault beaches inland.** NARA, Signal Corps photo

Left: **A tank dozer leads an armored column through Malmedy, Belgium, on 13 January 1945, clearing snow where necessary. The tank dozer was not a particularly good plow as deep snow mounded up quickly in front of the straight-on blade.** NARA, Signal Corps photo

overloaded the front suspension system and increased maintenance demands.

The army before D-Day requisitioned three hundred ninety M4s equipped with dozer blades, and one hundred five arrived in time for the landings. The D-Day tank battalions hit the beach with four each, and U.S Twelfth Army Group thereafter allocated the vehicles as they became available on the basis of six per tank battalion. The 738th Medium Tank Battalion, Special (Mine Exploder) had a custom allotment of four per tank company. Battalions In Italy typically had only two tank dozers; as of August 1944, the entire 1st Armored Division had only nine.

Tank dozers filled an incredible range of roles in Europe. On the D-Day beaches, they removed beach obstacles, opened roads, and pushed off beached landing craft. In Normandy, they were used to breach hedgerows to allow tanks to pass and even to bury German fighting positions on the opposite side. During the Siegfried Line fighting, tank dozers covered firing embrasures of occupied pillboxes and entrances of captured bunkers after the GIs learned the Germans would reoccupy them. Tank dozers removed roadblocks and wrecked vehicles, cleared rubble, dug positions for armored vehicles and guns, plowed up antipersonnel mines on road shoulders, and even cleared snow.[lxxxi]

The tank dozer's main roles in the Pacific Theater were constructing ramps for unloading LSTs, building roads, filling bomb craters, removing roadblocks, and closing caves. They were usually allocated on the basis of one per medium tank company.[lxxxii]

A tank dozer crashes through a hedgerow in Normandy on 13 July 1944. Experience showed that the dozers were capable of breaching about 50 percent of hedgerows. NARA, Signal Corps photo

*

The tank dozer was just a fighting with extra work. Sergeant Beetson commanded dozer-equipped tank 12, A/741st Tank Battalion, at Omaha Beach during the assault on D-Day and reported: "At 2,000 yards from shore, we began firing, expending about fifty rounds of HE ammunition. Landed on beach at approximately 0630 hours and continued firing at definite targets, both large gun and machine gun emplacements, using about ninety rounds HE ammunition. It is reasonably sure that hits were scored. During this time, we were also engaged in the removal of beach obstacles. At about noon, we reloaded with ammunition in order to continue with our work. At this time Lt. Klotz became a casualty due to enemy fire. The remainder

A 1st Armored Division tank dozer opens the way for a column in Italy in September 1944. This vehicle is a bit unusual as the dozer blade is attached to an M4A1. NARA, Signal Corps photo

of the crew continued the work of clearing the beach. It was necessary for the crew to dismount under fire to facilitate the removal of obstacles, which were dragged by means of cables. From time to time the crew assisted in the evacuation of wounded to the landing boats also while under fire. In the early afternoon, Sgt. Daum became a casualty due to enemy fire. The remainder of the crew continued operating the tank dozer, clearing the beach of obstacles, and the removal of wreaked and burning vehicles, in order to expedite the movement of traffic. This work was continued until the tide rendered further operations impossible."[lxxxiii]

Colonel William Triplet, commanding CCA, 7th Armored Division, described how he used tank dozers in January 1945 to force a path for his armor when the Ardennes snow was too deep for even tanks to maneuver: "The move shortly developed into an advance on a single tank front, the four tank dozers in column leading up the 2-kilometer slope to the middle between Auf der Hardt and Am Stein. The front dozer skimmed the top foot of snow; the snow would pile up in a large bow wave. It would then turn off to one side, pushing its load of snow off the main route, and the second dozer would then take the lead, followed by numbers three and four, while the former leader took place at the end of the dozer column."[lxxxiv]

FLAMETHROWERS

The flamethrower was an excellent weapon for clearing fortified positions, and the tank looked like a promising means to get one close to a bunker full of soldiers shooting back. Presumably inspired by the British "Crocodile" flamethrower, mounted on the Churchill tank, the U.S. Army in 1943 asked the British to build one hundred on the Sherman chassis. U.S. Headquarters, ETO, received four Crocodile-style Shermans in early 1944; these were eventually deployed by the 739th Medium Tank Battalion, Special (Mine Exploder), but the overall project was dropped by August. The Sherman Crocodile used a large capacity tube mounted on the side to ignite and deliver the fuel, which was carried in a 400-gallon trailer.

The history of the 739th records the first use of its Crocodile platoon in battle on 23 February 1945 while attached to the 29th Infantry Division: "The platoon moved to the Roer River opposite Jülich and received orders to cross the Roer, move into Jülich, and flame the citadel, the only remaining German resistance in said town. Two flamethrowing tanks advanced to within 75 yards of the citadel and began flaming and firing their 75mm guns at

One of only four Sherman Crocodiles to enter American service. The nozzle is to the right of the bow gunner's hatch, and the trailer carries the fuel. U.S. Army photo, records of the Armored Board

the steel door. The shots from the 75mm tore the doors down, and the flames drove defending infantry into tunnels, enabling the 175th Infantry Regiment to enter the citadel and wipe out remaining resistors." The third Crocodile, meanwhile, had broken its trailer pintle wires, and the fourth had driven into a shell hole.

*

The army decided to use a kit that it could install in fielded tanks instead of building specialized Crocodiles. The E4-5 equipment selected for use put a nozzle in the place of the hull machine gun, and the storage tanks containing compressed air and 50 gallons of the fuel sat behind the bog, who operated the weapon.[lxxxv] This system was capable of using crankcase oil mixed with gasoline, Napaline mixed with gasoline, or British fuel.[lxxxvi] The E4-5 was procured on the basis of nine units per tank battalion (a goal never achieved), and separate battalions were given first priority. The 70th Tank Battalion served as the test bed and received its first four units on 11 September 1944, and by November some eight more battalions had flame tanks.

*

Tankers in the ETO were divided over the utility of the E4-5 flamethrowers, which an AAR of the 743d described as "calculated to make the enemy burn with more than embarrassment." One tanker who fielded the hardware in the 70th recalls having used it to good effect against pillboxes.[lxxxvii]

The AAR for the 741st Tank Battalion, however, recorded for 18–19 September, "A flamethrower tank was used on one pillbox, but flamethrower had to approach within 20 yards of the box, and even then the flame was very unsatisfactory." Tankers in the 747th realized that the flamethrower and the German bazooka had similar ranges, which made them loath to

use the gear in battle against strongpoints. The equipment eliminated the cannon ammunition rack behind the assistant driver—another drawback.[lxxxviii] Most outfits appear to have shared the view of the 737th Tank Battalion, recorded in its journal on 28 February 1945: "Executive officer 17th Armored Group at CP at 1000, discussed flamethrowers. [We] said we don't want any flamethrowers and would like to get rid of those we now have."

The Army finally conceded that there was virtually no evidence that the E4-5 had rendered a contribution in combat that could not have been achieved with the bow machine gun or a white phosphorous round. Separate battalions nevertheless continued to be issued flamethrowers for months, but the growing disfavor kept the E4-5 out of the armored divisions except for the 14th, which installed two in each tank battalion.[lxxxix]

*

The flamethrower got heavy use in the Pacific Theater, mainly against prepared positions and caves but

Diagram of the installation of the E4-5 flamethrower. From ETOUSA General Board report on special armored equipment

A Sherman assistant driver fires his bow-mounted flamethrower during a demonstration. This photo gives a good idea of the weapon's limited range, which often put the tank in as much danger as the target. NARA, Signal Corps photo

at times to flush troops from bamboo thickets and tall grass. Tank crews reported that the weapon was very effective and had a powerfully demoralizing effect on the enemy. Battalions used no set pattern of allocation, but between six and eight per medium tank company appears to have been typical.[xc] The 776th Amphibian

A 709th Tank Battalion E4-5 flamethrower in action near Zweifall, Germany, on 24 November 1944. This tank still has a "green dozer" hedgerow buster from Normandy. The wartime censor has blacked out unit markings. NARA, Signal Corps photo

Tank Battalion in October 1944 landed a single LVT(A)(1) on Leyte Island with a flamethrower installed in place of the main armament, but it went unused for want of targets, and this may have been the only army flamethrower amtank in the theater.

A post-war study in the Pacific Theater concluded that despite its utility in battle, crews viewed the bow flamethrower as hazardous. The equipment obstructed access to the escape hatch, cramped the bog, and interfered with gear shifting.[xci]

*

The 713th Tank Battalion, Armored Flamethrower, in the Pacific was equipped with Shermans in which the main gun was replaced by a navy flame weapon that fired through the old gun barrel. Normally, the battalion's companies were attached to standard tank battalions (or at times split among two battalions), and in combat, two or three flame tanks operated with a standard tank platoon.

The battalion used the E12-7R1 flamethrower supplied by a 280-gallon fuel tank. A 3/4-inch nozzle discharged burning fuel at a rate of 4.4 gallons per second to a range of 155 yards. The modified tank required a crew of only four men as no loader was needed. The flamethrower proved extremely effective against bunkers and caves and could clear an entire hillside with a full fuel load.[xcii]

*

A veterans' association history of the 713th describes a typical action on Okinawa: "On 11 May, the flamethrowers operated with infantry and standard tanks near Zebra Hill. The operation was highly successful. The next day, the flamethrowing tanks moved through the standard tanks to burn the town of Gaja and nearby high ground. One tank was credited with killing seventy-five to one hundred enemy soldiers."[xciii]

M4A3E2 JUMBO ASSAULT TANK

Ordnance in early 1944 ordered production of two hundred fifty-four up-armored M4A3s for use as assault tanks to support the infantry during the looming campaign in Europe. The M4A3E2, nicknamed the Jumbo, began reaching tank battalions in October 1944. The Jumbo carried between 4 and 5-1/2 inches of armor up front (the lower hull was somewhat thicker than the upper hull) and, combining armor and the gun mantlet, up to 13 inches of steel on the turret front.[xciv] The extra sloped armor gave the Jumbo better protection than the

German Tiger tank had. The added weight reduced the top speed slightly to 22 miles per hour, and track grousers were standard in order to better spread the burden and reduce ground pressure.

The Jumbo was armed with the 75mm gun, a choice consistent with its infantry-support mission. Some nevertheless were retrofitted in the field with the 76mm gun for more effective performance against German tanks.

*

The record demonstrates a certain futility in this armor race: although the Jumbos clearly took more punishment than stock Shermans, they nevertheless regularly fell prey to guns of 75mm and higher, bazookas, and mines. Belton Cooper, an ordnance officer with the 3d Armored Division, examined one Jumbo that had been hit by a German gun in early 1945: "Even with all its extra armor, the tank was penetrated twice by the high-velocity German antitank projectiles. The first penetration was in the upper-right-hand corner of the tank where the reinforced glacis plate, side sponson, and top deck came together. . . . The next penetration struck the gun mantlet on the right side near the gunner's telescopic sight. It penetrated the 4-inch mantlet, then passed through 5 inches of armor near the gun trunnion and entered the turret."[XCV]

A Sherman with a bow-mounted flamethrower fires at a Japanese-occupied cave on Okinawa in June 1945. The relatively short range was not a problem in the Pacific because the Japanese lacked the bazooka-type weapons fielded by the Germans, which could kill a tank at about the same distance. NARA, Signal Corps photo

MINE CLEARING

American formations used special mine-clearing tanks on a very limited basis, mainly because they were most effective only under ideal conditions, whereas combat engineers worked effectively pretty much whenever they were told to. The most important type used a flail on a rotating drum suspended in front of the tank to detonate mines. The British deployed the first generation used in battle—dubbed the Scorpion—in North Africa at El Alemein. The flailing drum was spun by a separate engine mounted on the right front side of the tank, and the arms holding the drum were fixed, which meant that the chains could lose contact with the ground in rough or undulating terrain. The U.S. Army acquired several Scorpions and used them in Italy.

The Crab was an improvement of the basic design and served in some numbers with the Allies. Power for the drum, which had forty-three chains attached, was drawn from the tank's engine. The normal operating speed of the drum was 180 revolutions per minute, and the tank had an effective mine-clearing speed of 5 miles per hour. The booms could be raised and lowered, and the assembly added some 3,000 pounds to the vehicle. The improved Crab II had a contouring device that automatically raised and lowered the booms to follow the terrain.

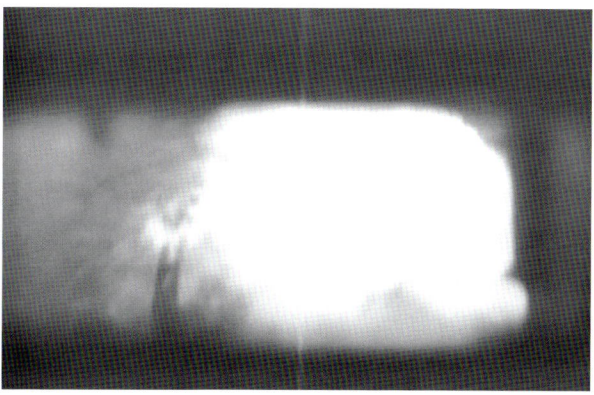

Periscope view from inside a Sherman of a bow flamethrower in action against a Japanese bunker. The gunner had to aim by watching where the flames hit. NARA, Signal Corps film

The main armament flamethrower could burn out an entire hillside. Here, a tank from the 713th goes to work on Okinawa's Hill 178 on 21 April 1945. NARA, Signal Corps photo

An M4A3E2 Jumbo assault tank from the 737th Tank Battalion moves forward, probably near the Sauer River in January 1945. The mesh on the hull and turret is probably for affixing foliage for camouflage. NARA, 737th Tank Battalion records

A newly arrived M4A3E2 Jumbo in November 1944 offers a good view of the commander's cupola also found on the 76mm M4 turret. The added loader's hatch is closed. Note the massively armored turret front, including the gun mantlet. The seam from the extra glacis armor is visible in front of the hull hatches. NARA, Signal Corps photo

Nine American Crabs arrived in Normandy in July 1944. The flails supported the 747th Tank Battalion when it entered St. Lô but proved ineffective because of the amount of rubble on the ground, and the 2d Armored Division used three of them during Operation Cobra. Technical observers with the British reported that their more extensive use of the Crab in Normandy had resulted in clearing 80 percent of mines at a casualty rate of 50 percent.

American officers in the ETO again seriously examined the Crab in November 1944, and twenty were soon procured in the United Kingdom. As this was insufficient for requirements, another fifteen were borrowed from 21st Army Group.[xcvi]

The Army had two roller-type mine-clearing systems that were issued in greater numbers than the flails but worked even less well. The mine exploder T1E1 consisted of three yokes mounting six steel disks 4 feet in diameter attached to the front of an M32 tank recovery vehicle. The assembly weighed 32,270 pounds. The T1E3 consisted of two sets of eight-foot discs in a frame yoke attached to the front of an M4 Sherman. A chain drive that drew power from the drive sprocket aided maneuver, a necessity considering the contraption's 58,500-pound weight. Both systems detonated mines by ground pressure; the vehicles could only travel at 10 miles per hour, and mine clearing took place at 3 miles per hour. Both were road-bound and proved troublesome on curvy roads or those with cratering. They also created new craters, so tank dozers often worked with mine-clearing tanks to fill in the holes. The roller tanks were vulnerable to offset and delayed-fuse mines and did not effectively clear a continuous path equivalent to the width of the tank.

Most mine-clearing tanks were concentrated in the 738th and 739th Medium Tank Battalions, Special (Mine Exploder), which arrived on the Continent in October 1944. They in turn attached one company to each corps in the First and Ninth armies, respectively.[xcvii]

*

Belton Cooper, 3d Armored Division, witnessed an attack by two CCB task forces during the start of the Roer River offensive on 16 November 1944: "Each task force had one flail tank. As the flail tanks crested the hill, they passed through our infantry line directly into the minefields. Although the tanks had to contend not only with mines but with an extremely soggy field, they made an initial good showing. The flying chains detonated several mines, and the explosions created additional craters. But finally, due to the combination of the muddy fields and the fact that the horsepower needed to turn the flail took too much power away from the tracks, both flail tanks became mired in the mud. They made excellent targets and were soon knocked out."[xcviii]

One officer described battle conditions in a Crab from the inside:

> The impact of the chains on the ground threw up dust or mud, which made visibility very difficult. . . . The dust was sucked into the interior of the tank through the normal intakes, but although this reduced visibility inside the tank, it never affected the efficiency of the crews. . . .
>
> The detonation of a single Teller [antitank] mine had curiously little effect inside the tank. It was possible to hear the explosion, and the tank shuddered as a ship will when a depth charge goes off some considerable way from her. Under the turret lights, the dust-laden air became more turbulent, and the engine noise rose as revolutions increased with the raising of the rotor by the blast of the mine. . . .[xcix]

The history of the 739th Medium Tank Battalion, Special (Mine Exploder) records a typical operation with mine rollers, in this case by Company A attached to the 5th Armored Division near Simmerath, Germany, on 30 January 1945: "[First Platoon] consisted of two T1E3s and two tank dozers. One tank dozer was lost due to mines. Approximately twelve Riegal mines were exploded by rollers, and the tank dozer cleared the road of snow drifts

A Jumbo fires its 75mm gun at a target in Aachen during the pre-attack bombardment of the city in early October 1944. Note the extra width of the tracks thanks to grousers. National Archives, Signal Corps film

ranging from 2 to 8 feet in depth. The cannon fire from the 76mm gun of the tank dozer contributed directly to the surrender and capture of two enemy pillboxes and one concrete shelter."

Not satisfied with the Tiger-tank-thick glacis on the Jumbo, the 750th Tank Battalion poured a layer of concrete on top. The battalion had to use jackhammers to remove the concrete at the end of the war. National Archives, Signal Corps film

A 4th Armored Division Jumbo (76mm) leads a tank column in Germany. The M4A3E2 often took point because it had the best chance of surviving the first shot fired from ambush. NARA, Signal Corps photo

A Scorpion flail tank demonstration under way in North Africa in August 1943. Note the outboard engine on the right side that drove the drum. NARA, Signal Corps photo

The 737th Tank Battalion history describes that command's first use of Calliope in combat: "On the 9th of February [1945], we uncovered a new secret weapon in the form of a 4.5-inch rocket launcher mounted on five tanks of Company C. . . . It was planned that [Lt. Clarence] Alberding was to fire two volleys from each tank [of two] on a strongly fortified hill, then occupied by the Germans. However, after dumping one hundred twenty rounds on the Krauts, the infantry advanced so rapidly that the hill was captured before the second volley could be discharged. Lieutenant [Vernon] Spellman fired three volleys from each of the [three] tanks but was unable to observe the fire from his position. However, the infantry commanders reported results just short of amazing. Many POWs on this and subsequent occasions when the rockets were used expressed the opinion that our rockets launched from tanks were worse than artillery and were extremely demoralizing."

ROCKET LAUNCHERS

In early December 1944, Ordnance began to equip some tanks with turret-mounted multiple rocket launchers intended to provide high-volume area-saturation fire.[c] The fairly common T34 Calliope model consisted of a 60-tube 4.5-inch rocket launcher mounted on a frame above the turret, and the rockets had a range of 4,000 yards. Typically, about one company per battalion was outfitted with the launchers. The crew controlled the elevation using the main gun, to which an extension arm was attached. Much to the annoyance of the crews, initial models prevented firing the main gun unless the aiming arm was removed. More than one tank outfit objected to the loss of tanks in their primary role, the vulnerability of the launchers to damage, and the additional supply and maintenance headaches. Several separate tank battalions—with the backing of infantry commanders—dumped the launchers after only weeks of use.[ci]

The T1E1 mine roller never really worked well in practice and saw very little use in the field. When clearing mines, the tank retriever crew would fold the boom back into place over the hull. NARA, records of the Government Printing Office

The Crab flail tank provided by the British was the most important mine clearer in American service but was far from perfect. The British built some six hundred Crabs. NARA, Signal Corps photo

A 739th Tank Battalion (Mine Exploder) T1E3 "Aunt Jemima" (hint: stacked pancakes) clears a road near Beggendorf, Germany, in December 1944. Mud like that caked on the bogie assemblies was the main enemy of the design. NARA, Signal Corps photo

A Sherman fitted with the late-model T34 rocket launcher fires in March 1945. The elevating rod is fixed above the main gun barrel, which allowed the gunner to fire without disconnecting the launcher. NARA, Signal Corps photo

CDL TANKS

One project that never lived up to its promise was a special M3 Grant tank that mounted a spotlight in a special turret and was codenamed a Canal Defense light, or CDL. Developed by the British in 1939, the CDL project was shared with the United States in 1942 with the proviso that American forces would not use the equipment without checking with London first. Moreover, the components would be manufactured by different firms and assembled under military supervision in order to maintain secrecy.

The primary mission of CDL tanks was to provide illumination for aimed fire at night. Secondary missions included dazzling enemy soldiers with a flicker effect and protecting friendly foot troops in triangles of darkness formed between adjacent lights. British tests showed that under controlled conditions the flickering could prevent an antitank crew from hitting the special tank from nearly any range.

*

No CDL battalion was used in combat as such, ironically because the project was so secret that ground commanders did not know the CDLs were available and plan accordingly.[cii] A few CDL tanks were employed as standard spotlights late in the war to illuminate bridge sites to prevent sabotage or to assist combat engineers in their work. A Col. John Briar offered as part of the Army's official explanation for the near non-use of the CDL in the ETO, "Colonel Walter Burnside, CO of the 10th Armored Group, made intensive efforts to find a place and sponsoring headquarters in September, October, and November 1944 to use the CDL tank units in operation but was unsuccessful. The 'gizmos' were actually used by the 738th Tank Battalion at the Remagen [bridge]. . . . Lieutenant Olson, 738th Tank Battalion, led four CDLs on 8 March 1945 to Remagen, and finally on [12] March 1945, Lt. Olson and his crew became the first Americans to use the CDL in combat."[ciii]

Ninth Army reequipped Company B of the 739th Medium Tank Battalion, Special (Mine Exploder) with CDL tanks to illuminate bridging sites beginning 23 March. Third Army also used three platoons of CDL tanks from the 748th at St. Goar, Bad Salsig, and Mainz.

A 13 million-candlepower arc light projected through the vertical slit in the turret of the CDL tank. This U.S. Army CDL is based on an M3A1 medium tank. U.S. Army photo

Mechanized Cavalry

After losing most of its tanks to the new Armored Force in 1940, the cavalry adapted just enough to modern warfare to establish mechanized cavalry battalions. These units employed light armored vehicles, including the M3/M5 tank series, M8 armored cars, and M8 assault guns, but remained outside the Armored Force.

Mechanized cavalry saw some action in North Africa and first saw large-scale use in the ETO, where the battalions operated under different names depending on role: 26 mechanized cavalry squadrons were attached to separate mechanized cavalry groups, 13 mechanized cavalry reconnaissance squadrons fought as organic components of light armored divisions, 2 armored reconnaissance battalions belonged to the heavy armored divisions, and 42 cavalry reconnaissance troops served as organic elements of infantry divisions. The infantry divisions in other theaters and the 1st Armored Division in Italy likewise had mechanized cavalry battalions.

Elements of the 113th Cavalry Group operate in France in September 1944 with a typical mix of light armored vehicles and jeeps. The cavalry often worked with tank units in spearheading breakouts. NARA, Signal Corps film

Except during the races across France and Germany, mechanized cavalry battalions were usually unable to execute the fast-moving mission foreseen for them. Finding the enemy was not the problem; kicking him bodily out of known positions was, and the lightly armored cavalry could contribute little. A post war survey of 12 mechanized cavalry groups revealed that they had spent 10 percent of their time in offensive combat and 3 percent performing reconnaissance, as compared with 33 percent in defensive combat and the remainder conducting rear-area security and other such missions.[vii]

The M8 was fine for indirect fire, but practically lacking machine guns and with extremely thin armor it was extremely vulnerable in close combat on the highly lethal European battlefield. Private First Class Clarence Horn, 740th Tank Battalion, offers one anecdote: "I thought it was plenty rough to go up front in an M5, and don't you think I didn't raise all kinds of hell when I was put to spearheading in an M8. Our mission was to carry 82d Airborne Division doughboys on our tank. . . . Well, it was about 8 o'clock in the evening when we picked up our boys and started out. The night was very cold, and the snow was about 4 feet deep, which made the roads very slippery. [The officer in command] put the M8 in the lead. That was when my darkest moment came. I was in the first tank, with nothing to shoot but an assault gun with no [tank-style direct fire] sight. I guess they expected me to shoot from the hip. It was just before daylight when we ran into a Jerry roadblock. They started shooting at us from all sides with every kind of weapon the Jerries had. They shot some flares in the air, and that is when my tail feathers fell. My tank was hit on the sprocket with a bazooka, which knocked the track off. We dismounted. Before the tank commander could say, "Get!" we were already out."[cvii]

An M8 shells the Germans near Karlsbrun, Germany, in February 1945. Indirect-fire missions were fairly common for assault guns when they could be tied into an artillery unit's fire-control center. NARA, Signal Corps photo

The 1st Armored Division, while still in North Africa in November 1943, assigned M7 Priest self-propelled 105mm howitzers to its medium tank battalions as stop-gap assault guns, because it found the 75mm howitzer under-powered in combat. The 751st substituted M7s for its M8s when it reorganized as a standard tank battalion in December 1943 while in Italy. NARA, Signal Corps film

105mm SHERMAN

The M4 and M4A3 (105mm How.) were to most widely used American assault guns and served with all standard tank battalions. The Armored Force decided in February 1943 that it wanted to replace on an urgent basis the M8 assault guns then being issued to medium tank battalions with a Sherman carrying a 105mm howitzer.[cviii] The vehicles were standardized in August 1943 but were not yet available to field units when the standardized tank battalion was established one month later.

The 105mm assault gun resembled the usual medium tank in nearly all ways. The model M4 howitzer replaced the 75mm gun in the turret, mounted with a .30-caliber coaxial machine gun. The gun had no gyrostabilizer, and the turret had only a manual traverse mechanism. On late-production models, a commander's vision cupola provided all-around vision through six prismatic blocks. The bow and antiaircraft machine guns found on the medium tank were retained.

The howitzer could elevate 35 degrees and depress 10 degrees. The gun produced a muzzle velocity of 1,550 feet per second and could throw an HE round indirectly about 12,000 yards. In practice, crews found that the high trajectory of the round precluded accuracy when firing

An early Sherman assault gun with 105mm howitzer. This vehicle has a standard commander's hatch, which was replaced on later editions by a vision cupola. NARA, Signal Corps photo

directly at targets farther away than 1,000 yards. The HEAI round proved able to defeat heavy German tanks, but it had an erratic flight path that made accuracy problematic at ranges longer than a few hundred yards.

The tank had stowage for sixty-six 105mm rounds (crews often squeezed in several more than that), plus 4,000 for the .30-calibers and three hundred for the .50-caliber. Each assault gun was allocated an M10 ammunition trailer to haul an additional fifty-four 105mm rounds, but combat units appear to have almost uniformly abandoned the trailers because they were a hindrance to maneuver and posed a risk of exploding under enemy fire.

This group of tanks on Okinawa includes very late-production assault guns equipped with HVSS suspension (center rear). The crews have all blotted out the white stars on the hull sides as they provided aiming points for Japanese gunners. Note the sandbags on the rear decks, which was standard practice in the Pacific because satchel charges and magnetic mines delivered by suicide squads rather than bazookas constituted the main close-range threat. NARA, Signal Corps photo

Assault guns from the 750th Tank Battalion fire indirectly in support of the 75th Infantry Division near Manhay, Belgium, on 30 December 1944. The battalion was in reserve, but the assault guns could still contribute to the battle. NARA, Signal Corps photo

The six guns per tank battalion could function as an armored artillery battery, and occasionally they were attached as such to an artillery unit. In separate tank battalions, the assault guns normally could fire indirectly only if the infantry division to which the outfit was attached took the trouble to integrate them into its fire direction system. This was never a problem in the internally integrated armored divisions.

*

Crew interviews conducted at the end of the war indicated general satisfaction with the 105mm assault gun, except for the lack of power traverse. That one shortfall made crews reluctant to use their tanks in direct-fire roles.[cix]

The after-action report of the 741st Tank Battalion for 11 July 1944 offers one vignette of the assault gun in the close-support role: "Lieutenant Colonel Norris, commanding the 2d Battalion, 38th Infantry, reported to Captain James G. Thornton Jr., commanding Company B, that his unit

A litter of empty shell containers surrounds a 736th Tank Battalion assault gun firing in support of the 83d Infantry Division in Neuss, Germany, on 3 March 1945. The gun's elevation suggests it has been shooting in direct support of the doughs, as does the heavy sandbagging. This tank has the commander's vision cupola with the single hatch. NARA, Signal Corps photo

A Soviet officer in April 1942 examines a 2d Armored Division Halftrack 81mm Mortar Carrier M4, based on the M2 halftrack. The shorter rear compartment and twin back steps are the easiest way to distinguish the M2 from the M3 halftrack. NARA, Signal Corps photo

was receiving fire from a camouflaged position south of a road junction on the St. Lô road. Captain Thornton ordered Lt. John A. Bruck, platoon leader of the assault gun platoon, to take the position out by direct fire. Lieutenant Bruck maneuvered one of his assault guns into position behind a house, which sat on the intersection facing the enemy position. The assault gun was placed in such a position that it could fire through the rear and front doors of the house directly into the German position. Several rounds were fired and flames and smoke spouted up from the target. Infantry patrols later reported that the position contained a Mark III assault gun and an antitank gun, both of which were completely demolished by the smashing impact of the 105mm projectiles."

Firing indirectly put assault guns at risk of counter-battery fire. Private First Class Flavian Kiracofe, 740th Tank Battalion, was with his assault gun platoon in Blatzheim, Germany, in early 1945: "We were set up there with no protection on our right flank. German tanks were firing on us, and a lot of big artillery was coming in. Jerry had zeroed in on the road that ran by our CP. He started knocking the houses down one by one. When he hit the

house next to the one we were in, I figured ours would be next. The thought of 'this is it' ran through my mind. We were on a fire mission at the time and had to stay with it. The forward observer was trying to adjust us in on the guns that were firing on us. We must have knocked them out for the shell earmarked for our house never did come in."[CX]

MORTAR CARRIERS

Headquarters Company included the mortar platoon—which delivered its punch from three 81mm mortars carried in halftracks—to provide close support to the line companies. The first vehicle issued, the Halftrack 81mm Mortar Carrier M4, was standardized in October 1940. As with later models, six men crewed the vehicle, and the mortar, which could throw its round 3,288 yards, was mounted in the bed of an M2 halftrack facing to the rear. Although the weapon could be fired from the vehicle in emergencies, the crew was supposed to dismount the weapon under normal circumstances. An improved model, the M4A1, was standardized in December 1942 and sported a stronger bed that allowed

the mortar to fire routinely from within the vehicle. Each M4 variant was also equipped with a .30-caliber machine gun that could be mounted on the gun rail or on a tripod, a bazooka, and one submachine gun.

The Halftrack 81mm Mortar Carrier M21, based on the M3 halftrack, entered service in July 1943. The mortar was repositioned to fire forward, and a .50-caliber machine gun on a pedestal mount replaced the .30-cal. The M21 carried 97 mortar rounds, a mixture of hand grenades, and twelve antitank mines. The halftrack featured either the SCR-509 or SCR-510 radio.

*

The 778th Tank Battalion's AAR for December 1944 offers a glimpse into the activities of a mortar platoon: "[The platoon] was attached to Company D and was instrumental on several occasions in assisting the advance of the infantry by placing fire on enemy gun positions and strongpoints that could not effectively be fired upon by other supporting weapons. . . . The mortar platoon, from advantageous positions on the west side of the Saar

The crew fires the weapon mounted in the Halftrack 81mm Mortar Carrier M4A1, which had a raised and strengthened floor mount designed to absorb the stress. NARA, Signal Corps photo

Below: **An M4A1 mortar crew in action near Overloon, Holland, in October 1944. Crews often turned the mortar to face forward so the vehicle could easily pull into position and begin firing.** NARA, Signal Corps photo

River placed harassing fire on the city of Bous, on the east side of the river. The platoon fired an average of three hundred fifty to four hundred rounds per day into the city. . . . The attachment of the mortar platoon to Company D in its reconnaissance and patrol work has proved very successful and has worked out to be by far the best use to which this platoon could be put. From one position on high ground at Bisten, mortars—firing at ranges up to 2,600 yards with HE light, medium, and smoke—neutralized fire from two groups of buildings, silenced two heavy gun positions, drove the enemy into woods, followed them with fire, and effected many casualties."

The 746th Tank Battalion in early 1945 found another use for its M4 or M4A1s: "We have found that the 81mm mortar platoon lends continuous fire support to advance infantry elements in many instances when tank fire cannot be employed successfully. The platoon. . . is attached to an infantry regiment and further attached to one battalion and the assault company thereof. By following closely behind the advancing infantry, the mobile mortars lay down covering fires within their maximum range before displacing to the next bound. In some actions, the mortar carriers have <u>backed</u> down the axis of advance from one bound to another."[cxi]

The crew of an 81mm Mortar Carrier T19, prototype for the M21, serves the weapon, which was designed to fire forward without the need for field expedients. NARA, records of the Chief of Ordinance

Despite such contributions, because of fire-control difficulties, the small number of tubes, and the tank commander's ever-improving ability to call for artillery support, the mortar platoon rarely played the role envisioned for it. By the end of hostilities, battalion commanders overwhelmingly viewed the mortars as superfluous.

Tank Crew

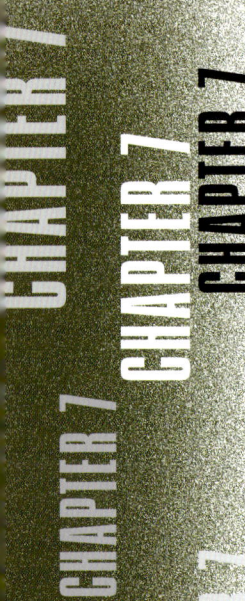

Tank battalion men were like the rest of the Army, mostly draftees and from all walks of life and corners of the nation. If a tanker was black, he served in a segregated separate tank battalion, where many of his officers were white. In the industrial war of the mid-twentieth century, these men were treated as replaceable parts, just as were their tanks, halftracks, and jeeps.

A lieutenant colonel commanded the tank, amtank, or amtrac battalion, assisted by an executive officer, who was normally a major. Captains filled staff jobs, such as operations officer (S-3), and commanded the line companies, while lieutenants ran the platoons. In battle, however, anything could happen in the company grades of tank battalions. Casualties often left lieutenants in command of companies and sergeants in charge of platoons. This in turn frequently led to a field promotion for the man involved, eventually.

An officer commanded his own tank, and otherwise a sergeant or a corporal normally commanded the crew;

privates, however, often were in charge of an amtrac. The men had little choice but to get along like a family because they spent so much time together, often cooped up in tight quarters. Perhaps even more than the GI in his foxhole, they depended on each other completely in battle, as each man's efficiency was needed to survive and a bad mistake by one could doom them all. Lieutenant Homer Wilkes related one simple example of a tank commander reacting instantly out of implicit trust in his crew. Wilkes's tank had just arrived at a line of departure in Normandy, where he could see no friendly infantry:

[William] Seaton, the driver, said, "Fire three HE fuse quick 50 feet straight ahead."

There were fruit trees in the area, hence the driver could see what I could not. I told the gunner to comply.

"What was it?" I asked afterward.

"A bazooka team was fixing to fire at us," replied Seaton.[cxii]

Above: **Commander and staff, 2/13th Armored Regiment (left), brief probably company and detachment commanders on the day's plan in North Africa. A map rests against the side of the command halftrack.** NARA, Signal Corps film

Left: **Tankers drove their home around with them. Often, sleeping quarters were no more than a shallow trench with the tank parked on top; tankers crawled in and out through the belly escape hatch. This assault gun crew from the 191st Tank Battalion is enjoying relatively luxurious digs.** NARA, Signal Corps photo

Technician Fourth Grade Robert Russo, a driver in a 740th Tank Battalion Sherman, related at war's end his crew's first real contact with the enemy during the Battle of the Bulge in Belgium:

On that particular night we were advancing down a road with the 30th Infantry Division, with Lt. Oglensky in the lead. We heard him call back to tell the battalion commander that it was getting too dark and too cloudy to go any farther, but the answer was to "keep pushing." Just about dark, Lt. Oglensky hit a tank mine, and he

Battalion Manpower

The manning of the various types of armored battalions changed over the course of the war, but never by huge amounts. As the reorganizations of 1943 were the most important, the following table offers a good basis of comparison among battalion types. (Note Off's=officers, WOs=warrant officers, and EM=enlisted men)

Personnel Strength
(1943 Tables of Organization and Equipment)

	Off's	WOs	EM
Tank Battalion (17-25):	39	2	709
Tank Battalion, Medium, Special (17-45S)	32	2	669
Tank Battalion, Light (17-15)	34	2	513
Amphibian Tank Battalion (17-115):	33	1	472
Amphibian Tractor Battalion (17-125):	33	4	750

immediately set up a roadblock with his tank. We were sixth or seventh tank back, so I thought we would spend a peaceful night. I was wrong! I was just about dozing off when all hell broke loose. I heard a large explosion, followed by another, and still another, and looking out the periscope I saw that three tanks in front of me were burning fiercely. Through my mind ran the thought of my trapped buddies, and you can imagine how I felt.

From that moment on, everything seemed to be a madhouse. I could see figures running back and forth, silhouetted by the flames of the burning tanks. I could swear Krauts were swarming all over our tank. A mortar hit just about where the transmission meets the hull of the tank and blew our gunner's helmet off. He had been looking out of the turret to find out where in hell all the firing was coming from. Someone jumped on our tank and yelled to Willie Morris, our tank commander, that the firing was coming from a chateau on our left flank.

I remember our loader, Corp. Waddell, feeding rounds into the gun as quickly as our gunner fired. He did a good job of keeping all the guns firing, and when he jerked the co-ax from its mount when it was too hot to fire any more I noticed his hands were bleeding, but he didn't seem to notice it. When next I looked out of the periscope, I saw that the Jerries were throwing flares right over our tank. I don't know to this day what actually kept us from getting hit. Maybe it was the wonderful coordination of our tank commander, gunner, and loader.[cxiii]

Men knew their platoon-mates well and the men in the company almost as well. Especially in the separate tank battalions, men from other companies were little more than strangers because the battalions were hardly ever together as units once committed to battle.

CREW KIT

The tanker had little personnel gear to keep track of, starting with his simple one-piece herringbone twill coverall that even had a built-in belt. He had his boots; a tanker's leather helmet and a steel pot; a tanker jacket, gloves, and bib-style overalls if the climate demanded; a bedroll, a mess kit; and a few other odds and ends. Tank crews in the Pacific found the herringbone twill coveralls too hot for use, and regular fatigues provided one solution. Men often fought stripped to the waist there, which increased the danger of severe burns from hot metal.[cxiv]

For trips outside the tank in battle, the commander had the submachine gun, usually the famous Tommy gun but late in the war often the M3 grease gun. Both were powerful .45-caliber weapons accurate only at short distances. Other crewmen typically were authorized a .45-caliber pistol (late war models such as the M4 series [76mm], M4 105mm assault gun, and M24 light tank provided all crewmen with submachine guns). All these weapons were considered battalion equipment furnished to the vehicle as part of its stowage list.[cxv] Accounts are remarkably common of tankers having to use their submachine guns, and hand grenades too, against enemy infantry.

Tankers sport herringbone twill coveralls, which was the basic tanker garment. Two of the Sherman crewmen have the dust-caked face that identifies them as the driver and "bog," who normally rode with their heads out of their hatches on road marches. Library of Congress, Prints & Photographs Division, FSA-OWI Collection

As the war dragged on, particularly in Europe where there were more potentially useful items to "liberate," crews tended to gather common property to make day-to-day life more comfortable. Lieutenant Colonel George Rubel, who commanded the 740th Tank Battalion, offered this observation regarding his crews during the Battle of the Bulge: "In [the] attack a tank was a strange looking object. There were usually from ten to twenty men riding on top of it. It was usually towing a trailer loaded down with rations, machine guns, tripods, and the usual miscellany of gear that a combat soldier takes along with him. In addition, the tankers had placed sandbags on the front slope plate of the tank, the sides, and sometimes around the turrets for protection against panzerfausts. Add to this conglomeration the tankers' housekeeping tools, which usually included a liberated heating stove, three or four

A crew in olive drab coveralls and tanker jackets loads 75mm ammunition into an M4. The black-tipped shells are AP, and the silver-tipped ones are HE. The gizmo on the Sherman's fender is a siren, which was sometimes used to signal an **attack.** NARA, Signal Corps photo

The leather tank helmet introduced in late 1941 had adjustable clamps to hold the earphones in place; a separate throat mike plugged into the intercom system. These coveralls have large pockets (not all did), a feature that annoyed some tankers because they snagged on protruding equipment in the tank. NARA, Signal Corps photo

Supporting Elements

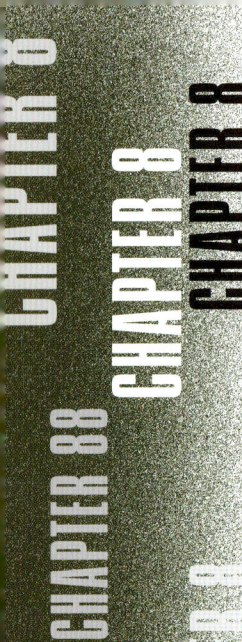

In tank battalions after 1942, Headquarters and Headquarters Company, Service Company, and a small medical detachment that reported to the battalion commander, kept the men and tanks running. The key pieces of motorized equipment in their operations were the jeep, the halftrack, the "deuce-and-a-half" 2-1/2-ton truck, and the tank recovery vehicle.[cxix]

While the tank battalion commander in an armored division was often in his tank with his unit in the field, in separate tank battalions the commander and his staff usually conducted their business in halftracks and jeeps. (Indeed, by late in the war they had become in many cases little more than an administrative headquarters that had little contact with their scattered line companies.) The battalion medical detachment operated one or two halftrack or 3/4-ton truck ambulances and several jeeps to pick up wounded tankers. Headquarters dispatch riders used motorcycles during the campaign in North Africa.

Headquarters Company's reconnaissance platoon consisted of only twenty-four men, whose main jobs

Above: **A halftrack and dispatch rider from 2/13th Armored Regiment in North Africa in November 1942. Jeeps became available in huge numbers and soon replaced motorcycles for many tasks.** NARA, Signal Corps film

Left: **The M29 light cargo carrier, known as the Weasel, was not standard issue but served with some battalions in the Pacific Theater, where it could claw through mud and over narrow hilly tracks.** NARA, Signal Corps photo

Storing maps in a reconnaissance jeep in North Africa in November 1942. Recon men were less well protected than just about everything else on the battlefield and tried to avoid situations where they had to use the machine gun. NARA, Signal Corps film

were road reconnaissance prior to marches and securing any tank company lacking infantry support at night, although they also conducted some combat reconnaissance missions. Initially, the platoon used motorcycles, but by the landings in North Africa standard equipment consisted of one halftrack and five jeeps. In the standardized tank battalion, light tanks from Company D were sometimes used to buttress the recon platoon.

This tank battalion from the 66th Armored Regiment, 2d Armored Division, is gathered at a marshalling area on 29 May 1944. The photo shows tanks with and without wading gear, halftracks, deuce-and-a-half cargo trucks, a T2 tank recovery vehicle, and a non-standard-issue 1/4-ton amphibian truck.
NARA, Signal Corps photo

1st Armored Division men in winter uniforms stand next to "Bantam cars" in early 1941. Bantam for some reason later argued that the jeep design copied the company's product.
NARA, Signal Corps photo

Service Company ran a fleet of jeeps and 2-1/2 ton trucks to supply food, fuel, lubricants, and other necessities to the tank companies. It also fielded tank recovery vehicles to augment the one normally assigned to each tank company.

Standard battalions about to engage in an amphibious or river-crossing operation might be issued a few non-standard amphibious trucks. Tank battalions in the Pacific Theater faced tropical rains and mud, and some used the tracked M29 "Weasel" on a limited basis and liked them well.[cxx]

Headquarters and support units in amphibian battalions resembled those in land units in organization and function. Support equipment actually used in the amphibian armored units was a more ad hoc affair, depending on circumstances. The maintenance section, for example, was authorized a standard wrecker for use while the battalion was ashore, but it had an extremely low shipping priority, and one veteran commented, "I never saw it."[cxxi]

WHEELED VEHICLES

The incredibly versatile jeep, as the 1/4-ton truck is popularly known, was called a "peep" in the Armored Force and was used widely by combat and support elements in tank and (when ashore) amphibian armored units. The Armored Force began receiving "Bantam reconnaissance cars" in 1941, but the Quartermaster Corps meanwhile was contracting with Willys to deliver a suspiciously similar light truck. Ordnance took over the project in 1942, and the jeep took its place in American military lore. The 1/4-ton designation meant that the jeep could carry that much cargo weight.

The jeep weighed 3,253 pounds, and its four-cylinder, 54 horsepower gasoline engine could move the vehicle at a speed of 65 miles per hour on level ground. Equipped with four-wheel drive, the jeep could climb a 60-percent slope. A base plate was provided for a pedestal mount to accommodate a machine gun, which was installed, for example, in reconnaissance jeeps. A .30-caliber machine gun could also me mounted above the dashboard or outboard in front of the passenger.

The new 1/4-ton truck being put through its paces in March 1941. The vehicle was unstable at high speed and had a nasty tendency to roll over. NARA, Signal Corps photo

*

The "deuce-and-a-half" cargo truck was the second great automotive development of the war. The six-wheel-drive vehicle weighed 15,450 pounds and had a six-cylinder, 94 horsepower engine governed to permit a maximum speed of 45 miles per hour on level ground. The truck naturally was rated to carry 2-1/2 tons of cargo but in practice was often burdened with up to 10 tons, which forced maintenance crews to replace engines as often as every 10,000 miles.[cxxii]

A Dodge 3/4-ton truck was used in lesser numbers as a weapons carrier and as an ambulance. In the pre-standardized tank battalion, a 3/4-ton truck mounting a 37mm gun (apparently identical to the M6 tank destroyer) was included in the administrative, supply, and mess section of battalion and probably tank company head-quarters. The Dodge vehicle had a six-cylinder, 76 horse power gasoline engine and could reach a maximum speed of 54 miles per hour.

*

An armored unit jeep fitted out for reconnaissance in early 1945 carries a pedestal-mounted .30-caliber machine gun. In sunnier climates, the wind screen was usually lowered so that sunlight would not glint off the glass and alert the enemy.
NARA, Signal Corps film

A jeep, probably from the battalion headquarters of 2/13th Armored Regiment, in North Africa. The machine gun is mounted forward rather than on a pedestal in the rear compartment. NARA, Signal Corps film

Tank battalions could not have fought without the Service Company men, whose job was plenty dangerous even though they were not front-line combat troops. They had to work in range of enemy guns in soft-skinned vehicles often filled with ammunition or gasoline.

Consider the accounts of several such soldiers. Joseph Fetch offered philosophically, "Delivering gas to the front was a little hairy, but I never had a problem. They'd say, 'Get that damn gas truck out of here.' All you'd need was a piece of shrapnel to hit one can, and I'm sitting there with a 2-1/2-ton truck, no canopy or no top on it. Three hundred cans, five gallons apiece, about 1,500 gallons of gasoline, and just one little piece of shrapnel, and I'm sitting on dynamite."[cxxiii]

Private First Class John Gerlock recalled, "The second squad of the mortar platoon was attached to Service Company. We were helping them to load ammunition when shells started to come in, but going quite a bit over us. Some of the boys were fixing flat tires on their trucks, but some of the tires were torn up so bad that they were beyond repair. Lieutenant Otto knew where

there were some Jerry tires, and he asked for two volunteers to go with him to get them. . . . We were going OK until the enemy spotted us, and then we really caught hell. For three hours we were shelled, but fortunately none of us was hit. We got our tires, and the trucks were able to go."

Sergeant Avrie Humphrey remembered, "Our first platoon was out of ammunition and somehow we had to get it to them. In doing so we had to go across a great deal of open country. We eased the peep along as easy as we could in hopes that Jerry wouldn't see us until we got across. That is where we made our worst mistake. Jerry must have been watching us, because just as we hit the open road he opened up on us with his mortars. When the first round hit we knew he had seen us, so we left the peep for a more suitable place in a nearby ditch. After the mortars stopped, we mounted the peep and tried again, but it was the same old story. This time they were a lot closer, and I was sure my number was up. But we decided to try again. Jerry slung them at us again, but by this time I was already in a daze, so we kept on going.

After we had given the platoon their ammunition, we had to go through the whole thing again."

Sergeant Leo Havens reckoned, "My darkest moment was one day when I was following the tanks up trying to get a long enough break to repair a radio. . . . We had just stopped for a moment, and I was sitting in my peep behind a light tank when a flak wagon opened up on us. I dove from the peep into the ditch in one leap. As I hit the ditch, they started firing up it, and every time I would move up (and I was moving!), a shell would burst where I had been a moment before."[cxxiv]

Testing the 2-1/2-ton truck at Aberdeen Proving Grounds in July 1941. The twin front tires on the front axel were not employed in the field. NARA, Signal Corps photo

HALFTRACKS

The halftrack could carry men, equipment, and supplies almost any place a tank could go and could mount an array of machine guns. The first model to reach tank battalions was the M2, standardized in 1940, which weighed 19,800 pounds and had a six-cylinder gasoline engine that could move it along at 40 miles per hour. The halftrack carried 60 gallons of fuel and had a cruising range of 175 miles. Various radios could be mounted in the vehicle as needed.

Armor plating 1/4-inch thick protected the entire vehicle except for a hinged 1/2-inch plate that could be swung down over the windshield. The armor was calculated to be stout enough to stop small-arms fire, but the halftrack earned a very bad name among the troops regarding protection as early as the fighting in North Africa. One soldier, when asked by an officer if German aircraft bullets would go through the halftrack, replied, "No, sir. They only come through one wall and then they rattle around."[cxxv]

The M2 had a short bed and could transport ten men when equipped with seats in the cargo space. A gun rail ran around the upper wall of the cargo area and typically supported three machine guns; the layout precluded a back door, so men had to mount and dismount over the walls.

The M3 halftrack was essentially the same vehicle fitted out

A 2d Armored Division 3/4-ton ambulance on a road in France in September 1944. Casualties were usually evacuated by hand or by jeep to a forward aid station and only then, perhaps, be transferred by ambulance. NARA, Signal Corps film

A 3/4-ton weapon carrier mounting a 37mm gun (center), probably belonging to the battalion headquarters of 2/13th Armored Regiment in North Africa. A reconnaissance jeep is to the left, a deuce-and-a-half to the right, and an M3 medium tank behind the Dodge. NARA, Signal Corps film

with a longer bed and a rear door, and the new layout boosted hauling capacity to thirteen men. The M2A1 and M3A1 models added a ring mount for a .50-caliber machine gun over the passenger's seat in the cab. Several minor variants appeared under the designations M3A2, M5, M5A1, M5A2, and M9A1.

The weapon carrier mounting the 37mm gun also saw action in North Africa as the M6 tank destroyer, a role in which it proved woefully ineffective when confronted by German panzers. NARA, Signal Corps photo

Within the tank battalion, halftracks were used only in the support elements, and amphibian units did not use them at all. A command halftrack was available for the battalion commander or his operations officer to keep track of the action by radio, and the battalion surgeon normally had one fitted out as an ambulance. In broken terrain, halftracks at times deployed as radio relay stations between headquarters and the tanks.

*

The halftrack with its machine guns could be a formidable weapon under the right circumstances. One 1st Armored Division armored infantry officer told a visiting observer in early 1943, "During the engagement of 3-6 December, I used a platoon of halftracks to counterattack, employing them as tanks against a German company that had penetrated the front line and that had no antitank weapons. The attack was highly successful." He nevertheless added, "It is my opinion that the machine gun of the M3 halftrack is too high. We have had quite a number of gunners killed and wounded. I believe some sort of shield [should] be put on the gun."

TANK RETRIEVERS

The Army became remarkably adept at recovering, repairing, and reusing damaged tanks, which proved to be a tremendous force multiplier. The need in North Africa was critical, as replacement shortages multiplied the value of every piece of equipment as compared with Stateside and later theaters. Sadly, high attrition rates caused by high-velocity guns and various bazookas in the ETO also hiked the importance of field repairs. Tanks also were apt to throw tracks and suffer other mechanical problems simply in the normal course of events.

Tank battalions at first relied on the heavy wrecking truck, which came in several models. The M1 was essentially a civilian truck standardized in 1937; a modestly improved variant, the M1A1, entered service in 1944. The 38,500-pound M1 had six-wheel-drive and a six-cylinder, 133 horse power engine that produced a top speed of 45 miles per hour. A crane in the bed could be used to the rear or the sides and had a lifting capacity of 16,000 pounds. A rear winch could pull 37,500 pounds using a single steel cable, while a 20,000-pound capacity front winch was available to pull the truck free if it mired or to anchor the wrecker when pulling with the rear winch. The vehicle normally carried repair tools such as welding gear.

The wrecker was highly vulnerable on the battlefield, however, and could not go everywhere a tank could

The M2 had a rail around the rear compartment to which several machine guns could be fixed, in this case one .50-caliber pointing to the rear and two water-cooled .30-calibers facing forward. NARA, Signal Corps photo

The M3 had a slightly longer rear compartment, which created room for three more seats, and a pedestal-mounted machine gun. The M3 and its variants were the most widely used half-track in American service. NARA, Signal Corps photo

go, and the anticipated retirement of the M3 medium tank provided a solution. Ordnance in September 1942 ordered that 108 M3s be converted to tank retrievers by removing the 75mm and 37mm guns and installing a boom and 60,000-pound-capacity rear winch. Tank units almost always referred to the retriever by its developmental designation, the T2, although it was officially designated the M31 in November 1943. The first of 805 T2s built became available in North Africa by May 1943, and the vehicle remained in service through the war.

Fake guns were installed to give the appearance of a fighting tank, but the 75mm sponson was actually a door that provided easy entry and exit. Six men crewed the vehicle, which retained a .30-caliber machine gun in the bow and another in the turret, and crews often mounted another machine gun atop the turret. The T2 carried various repair tools such as welding gear.

The various models of M4 medium tank became available in such large quantities that some were converted to tank retrievers under the designation M32,

A 2d Armored Division T2 advances during Operation Cobra in July 1944. Note the extra .50-caliber machine gun atop the turret and what appears to be a .30-caliber below and to the right of that. NARA, Signal Corps photo

A T2 recovers a Sherman near Grosshau, Germany, in December 1944. Note the handle on the sponson door beside the fake 75mm gun, which was supposed to convince the enemy that the T2 was a battle tank. NARA, Signal Corps photo

A tank recovery vehicle T5E3 (development vehicle for the M32) displays the 81mm mortar when mounted. Accounts of the mortars being used in action are infrequent. NARA, U.S. Army photo

M2A1 and M3A1 halftracks added a ring mount for a .50-caliber machine gun. This enabled the gunner to acquire targets in a full 360-degree arc. NARA, Signal Corps photo

An M3 command halftrack at the Desert Training Center in November 1942. In practice, tank battalion commanders generally used a jeep in the separate battalions or a tank in the armored divisions. NARA, Signal Corps photo

occasionally referred to as the T5, which was standardized in October 1943. The M32 had hauling and lifting characteristics similar to those of the T2. It retained the Sherman's bow machine gun, carried a .50-caliber on the turret, and fielded an 81mm mortar that could be mounted on the front to lay down smoke to protect recovery operations—or on rare occasion to fire at the enemy.

*

Lieutenant Homer Wilkes of the 747th Tank Battalion recalled the T2 and its early contribution to the war in France, "The driver of this machine sat astride a five-speed, manual transmission. The clutch was on its left, the accelerator on the right. . . . The T2 was a remarkably good tank retriever. Its only drawback was a strange silhouette. Seeming to take it for some sort of secret weapon, the enemy would engage the thing with every weapon in his possession." Being a tank even if lacking main armament, the T2 could play a role in combat denied the heavy wrecker. On D-Day in Normandy, T/Sgt. Virgil Givins, 747th, commanding Company A's T2, carried Rangers on the back deck while exiting Omaha Beach

A 2d Armored Division ambulance passes through St. Amand, France, on 2 September 1944. The halftrack ambulance could follow the tankers places a wheeled ambulance could not go. NARA, Signal Corps film

The M1 6x6 wrecker with winch was the first tank retriever. It was poorly suited to hauling heavy tracked vehicles across muddy terrain and was vulnerable to enemy fire. U.S. Army photo

Bibliography

The American Arsenal. London: Greenhill Books, 2001. The Greenhill volume is essentially a reprint of the U.S. Army's Catalog of Standard Ordnance Items of 1944.

Anderson, Rich. "The United States Army in World War II." Military History Online. http://www.militaryhistoryonline.com/wwii/usarmy, 2000.

Cameron, Robert Stewart. Americanizing the Tank: U.S. Army Administration and Mechanized Development Within the Army, 1917-1943. Dissertation, Temple University, August 1944. UMI Dissertation Services: Ann Arbor, Michigan, 1996.

Cooper, Belton Y. Death Traps: The Survival of an American Armored Division in World War II. Novato, Ca: Presidio Press, Inc., 2000.

Elson, Aaron C. Tanks for the Memories: An Oral History of the 712th Tank Battalion from World War II. Hackensack, N.J.: Chi Chi Press, 1994.

Forty, George. Tank Warfare in the Second World War: An Oral History. London: Constable and Company Ltd, 1998.

Gilbert, Oscar E. Marine Tank Battles in the Pacific. Da Capo Press, 2001.

Green, Michael. M4 Sherman. Osceola, WI: Motorbooks International Publishers & Wholesalers, 1993.

Greenfield, Kent Roberts; Robert R. Palmer; and Bell I. Wiley. United States Army in World War II, The Organization of Ground Combat Troops. Washington, DC: Historical Division, Department of the Army, 1947.

Harmon, Ernest. Combat Commander. Englewood Cliffs, New Jersey: Prentice-Hall, Inc, 1970.

Heintzleman, Al. We'll Never Go Over-Seas. Self-published, 1982.

History and Role of Armor, ST 17-1-2, US Armor School, April 1974.

Houston, Donald E. Hell on Wheels, The 2d Armored Division. Novato, California: Presidio Press, 1977.

Irzyk, Lt. Col. Albin. "Assault Guns." Cavalry Journal, July-August 1945, 34-36.

Jensen, Marvin. Strike Swiftly: The 70th Tank Battalion from North Africa to Normandy to Germany. Novato, Ca.: Presidio Press, 1997.

Johnson, David E. Fast Tanks and Heavy Bombers, Innovation in the U.S. Army 1917-1945. Ithaca, NY: Cornell University Press, 1998.

Maddox, Eddie Jr. 736 Special Tank Battalion. Self-published, 2000.

Mesko, Jim. M3 Half-tracks in Action. Carrollton, Texas: Squadron/Signal Publications, Inc., 1996.

Miller, John Jr. United States Army in World War II, The War in the Pacific, Guadalcanal: The First Offensive. Washington, DC: Historical Division, Department of the Army, 1949.

Organization, Equipment, and Tactical Employment of Separate Tank Battalions. The General Board, United States Forces, European Theater, 14 May 1946.

Rubel, Lt. Col. George. Daredevil Tankers: The Story of the 740th Tank Battalion, United States Army. Göttingen, Germany: 740th Tank Battalion, 1945.

Sawicki, James A. Tank Battalions of the U.S. Army. Dumfries, Va.: Wyvern Publications, 1983.

Spearhead in the West. Frankfurt, Germany: 3d Armored Division, 1945.

Triplet, William S. A Colonel in the Armored Divisions. Columbia, Missouri: University of Missouri Press, 2001.

VandenBergh, Maj. William J. "Executing the Double Retrograde Delay: The 194th Tank Battalion in Action During the Luzon Defense Campaign 1941-42," Armor, November-December 2002, 26-31.

Wilkes, Homer D. 747th Tank Battalion. Scottsdale, Arizona: self-published, 1977?
    APO 230. Scottsdale, Arizona: self-published, 1982.
    Sitrep. Scottsdale, Arizona: self-published, 1981.

Zaloga, Steven, Terry Handler, and Mike Badrocke. Amtracs. Botley, UK: Osprey Publishing Ltd., 1999.

Zumbro, Ralph. Tank Aces. New York, NY: Pocket Books, 1997.

Endnotes

Chapter 1: History of the Armored Battalions

i James A. Sawicki, *Tank Battalions of the U.S. Army* (Dumfries, Va.: Wyvern Publications, 1983), 32 and *passim*. Steven Zaloga, Terry Handler, and Mike Badrocke, *Amtracs* (Botley, UK: Osprey Publishing Ltd., 1999), 13.

ii Robert Stewart Cameron, *Americanizing the Tank: U.S. Army Administration and Mechanized Development Within the Army, 1917-1943* (Dissertation, Temple University, August 1944. UMI Dissertation Services: Ann Arbor, Michigan, 1996), 492-493. Donald E. Houston, *Hell on Wheels, The 2d Armored Division* (Novato, California: Presidio Press, 1977), 33-34.

iii Cameron, 492-493. Houston, 33-34.

iv Cameron, 492-493.

v Cameron, 493. David E. Johnson, *Fast Tanks and Heavy Bombers, Innovation in the U.S. Army 1917-1945* (Ithaca, NY: Cornell University Press, 1998), 121.

vi Cameron, 494. Houston, 35.

vii Cameron, 495ff. Kent Roberts Greenfield, Robert R. Palmer, and Bell I. Wiley, *United States Army in World War II, The Organization of Ground Combat Troops* (Washington, DC: Historical Division, Department of the Army, 1947), 6. Houston, 35. Marvin Jensen, *Strike Swiftly: The 70th Tank Battalion from North Africa to Normandy to Germany* (Novato, Ca.: Presidio Press, 1997), 7.

viii Memorandum from Chief of Ordnance to Gen. Jacob L. Devers, Chief, Army Field Forces, 3 August 1948, NARA, RG 337, Army Field Forces Headquarters, Box 9, folder 470.8. Greenfield, et al, 56–61, 321–326. Cameron, 521-522.

ix *History and Role of Armor*, ST 17-1-2, US Armor School, April 1974, 13. Cameron, 500.

x Jensen, 7-8.

xi Records of the 13th Armored Regiment.

xii Captain Arthur Rolph, "Battlefield Vehicle Recovery," *Armored Cavalry Journal*, July-August 1947, 46.

xiii Cameron, 495ff.

xiv Rich Anderson, "The United States Army in World War II." Military History Online. http://www.militaryhistoryonline.com/wwii/usarmy, 2000, as of February 2004. Unit Journal, 751st Tank Battalion, 4 March-9 April 1943.

xv FM 17-33, *The Armored Battalion*, September 1942, 7.

xvi Sawicki, 16.

xvii Anderson.

xviii *Armored Special Equipment*, The General Board, United States Forces, European Theater, 14 May 1945.

xix Anderson.

xx *Staff Officers' Field Manual for Amphibious Operations*, Fleet Marine Force, Pacific, 10 September 1944. Pacific Warfare Board Report No. 70, 5 October 1945, NARA, RG 94, 4-7.70/45, box 24464.

xxi "713th Flame Throwing Tank Battalion," The 11th Armored Division Association, www.11tharmoreddivision.com, as of January 2004. Pacific Warfare Board Report No. 76, 6 November 1945, NARA, RG 94, 4-7.76/45, box 24464.

xxii William S. Triplet, *A Colonel in the Armored Divisions* (Columbia, Missouri: University of Missouri Press, 2001), 46.

xxiii *History and Role of Armor*, 13. Cameron, 546ff. Johnson, 146-147.

xxiv Cameron, 540ff.

xxv *Tactics of Armored Units, the Tank Platoon*, Training Guide #1, Headquarters, Armored Force, 2 January 1942. See RG 337, box 341, NARA.

xxvi Cameron, 548ff.

xxvii Johnson, 120ff.

xxviii Cameron, 796.

xxix *Organization, Equipment, and Tactical Employment of Separate Tank Battalions*, The General Board, United States Forces, European Theater, 14 May 1946.

xxx Cameron, 521-522. Maj. William J. VandenBergh, "Executing the Double Retrograde Delay: The 194th Tank Battalion in Action During the Luzon Defense Campaign 1941-42," *Armor*, November-December 2002, 26-31.

xxxi Memorandum, "Operations of the Provisional Tank Group, United States Army Forces in the Far East—1941-1942," posted at http://bataanwashell.blog-city.com as of January 2004.

xxxii Memorandum, "Station List of the Armored Force," 16 December 1941, RG 337, box 341, NARA.

xxxiii Memorandum 461/135, "Reports," Adjutant General's office, GHQ, to CG, Armored Force, 12 December 1941. Memorandum 471/7(Armd Force)-H, "Allocation of Ammunition for Training," Headquarters Armored Force, 6 February 1942, Both in RG 337, box 341, NARA.

xxxiv Memorandum 475/1 (Armored Force) (12-31-41), "Shortage of Critical Items of Equipment in 1st and 2d Armored Divisions as of January 1, 1942," 1 January 1942, Misc Div AG Sec GHQ U.S. Army, RG 337, box 341, NARA.

xxxv Memorandum, "Availability of 3d and 4th Armored Divisions," Lt. Gen. L.J. McNair to CG, Field Forces, 14 January 1942,

xxxvi Memorandum, "Operations of the Provisional Tank Group, United States Army Forces in the Far East—1941-1942."

xxxvii Notes of Major General Omar Bradley on visit to the 1st Armored Division, 1 March 1943. Records of the 1st Armored Division.

xxxviii "Observer Report," 13 March 1943. Included in "Report of Observers: Mediterranean Theater of Operations," Volume 1, 22 December 1942-23 March 1943.

xxxix Jensen, 83.

xl Pacific Warfare Board Report No. 70, 5 October 1945, NARA, RG 94, 4-7.70/45, box 24464.

xli AARs, 708th Amphibian Tank Battalion.

xlii AAR for Leyte campaign, 776th Amphibian Tank Battalion.

xliii AAR, 780th Amphibian Tank Battalion.

xliv Pacific Warfare Board Report No. 66, 9 September 1945, NARA, RG 94, 4-7.60/45, box 24464.

xlv Pacific Warfare Board Report No. 66, 9 September 1945, NARA, RG 94, 4-7.60/45, box 24464. Pacific Warfare Board Report No. 72, 16 October 1945, NARA, RG 94, 4-7.72/45, box 24464.

xlvi Pacific Warfare Board Report No. 74, 26 October 1945, NARA, RG 94, 4-7.74/45, box 24464.

xlvii Pacific Warfare Board Report No. 13, 18 June 1945, NARA, RG 94, 4-7.13/45, box 24462.

Endnotes for Chapter 2: Light Tanks

xlviii Armored Force Board report 138, 30 June 1941, NARA, RG 156, Chief of Ordnance, Box J-358.

xlix Gilbert, 26.

l Jensen, 67.

li *Tank Gunnery*, The General Board, United States Forces, European Theater, not dated.

lii Memorandum from Col. Louis Heath to Col. G. M. Dean, Armored Vehicle Branch, Requirements Division, Army Ground Force, 23 August 1944, NARA, RG337, Armored Board, Box 79.

liii Lt. Col. E. A. Trahan, "Speed—The Essence of Armor," *Armored Cavalry Journal*, May-June 1947, 30.

liv Letter cited in monograph extract at Merriam Press's web site, www.Merriam-press.com/mono_200/m240-ex.htm.

Endnotes for Chapter 3: Medium Tanks

lv Al Heintzleman, *We'll Never Go Over-Seas* (Self-published, 1982), 2.

lvi *Spearhead in the West* (Frankfurt, Germany: 3d Armored Division, 1945), 41-42.

lvii Ralph Zumbro, *Tank Aces* (New York, NY: Pocket Books, 1997), 105.

lviii "Medium Tank Development," undated study, NARA, RG 156, Chief of Ordnance, Box J-730.

lix Ernest Harmon, *Combat Commander* (Englewood Cliffs, New Jersey: Prentice-Hall, Inc, 1970), 146.

lx Colonel Henry Gardiner, "We Fought at Kasserine," *Armored Cavalry Journal*, March-April 1948, 10.

lxi *Tank Gunnery*, The General Board, United States Forces, European Theater, not dated.

lxii Ernest Harmon, *Combat Commander* (Englewood Cliffs, New Jersey: Prentice-Hall, Inc, 1970), 115.

lxiii Ralph Zumbro, *Tank Aces* (New York, NY: Pocket Books, 1997), 108-109.

lxiv Homer D. Wilkes, *747th Tank Battalion* (Scottsdale, Arizona: self-published, 1977?), 44.

lxv Michael Green, *M4 Sherman* (Osceola, WI: Motorbooks International Publishers & Wholesalers, 1993), 102.

lxvi Johnson, 192-193.

lxvii *Tank Gunnery*, The General Board, United States Forces, European Theater, not dated.

lxviii George Forty, *Tank Warfare in the Second World War: An Oral History* (London: Constable and Company Ltd, 1998), 116-117.

Endnotes for Chapter 4: Amphibious Tanks

lxix William S. Triplet, *A Colonel in the Armored Divisions* (Columbia, Missouri: University of Missouri Press, 2001), 64.

lxx Pacific Warfare Board Report No. 70, 5 October 1945, NARA, RG 94, 4-7.70/45, box 24464. AAR for Operation Forager, 715th Amphibian Tractor Battalion.

lxxi Historical report, 718th Amphibian Tractor Battalion.

lxxii Lieutenant Russell A. Gugeler, "Army Amphibian Tractor and Tank Battalions in the Battle of Saipan 15 June-9 July 1944," U.S. Army Center of Military History, w w w . a r m y . m i l / c m h - pg/documents/wwii/amsai/amsai.htm as of May 2004.

lxxiii "Supplemental Report of Operations, Ormoc-Palompon Area, Camotes Islands Operations," undated report, records of the 718th Amphibian Tractor Battalion.

lxxiv William S. Triplet, *A Colonel in the Armored Divisions* (Columbia, Missouri: University of Missouri Press, 2001), passim.

lxxv AAR on the Leyte campaign, 776th Amphibian Tank Battalion. Memorandum, "Special Report of the Operation of the Provisional Armored group (Amphibious) with the 77th Infantry Division for the Period 26 March to 26 April 1945," Headquarters, Provisional Armored Group, 26 April 1945.

lxxvi *Army Amphibian and Tractor Training in the Pacific*, 1st Information and Historical Service, not dated.

lxxvii William S. Triplet, *A Colonel in the Armored Divisions* (Columbia, Missouri: University of Missouri Press, 2001), 48.

lxxviii AAR, 708th Amphibian Tank Battalion.

lxxix Memo by Major William Duncan, 743d Tank Battalion: "Results of Training, Tests, and Tactical Operations of DD Tanks at Slapton Sands, Devon, England, During Period 15 March - 30 April 1944," dated 30 April 1944 and contained in the records of the 753d Tank Battalion.

lxxx Al Heintzleman, *We'll Never Go Over-Seas* (Self-published, 1982), 26.

Endnotes for Chapter 5: Specials and Variants

lxxxi *Armored Special Equipment*, pp. 14ff.

lxxxii Pacific Warfare Board Report No. 72, 16 October 1945, NARA, RG 94, 4-7.72/45, box 24464.

lxxxiii Personal reports, records of the 741st Tank Battalion.

lxxxiv William S. Triplet, *A Colonel in the Armored Divisions* (Columbia, Missouri: University of Missouri Press, 2001), 179.

lxxxv *Armored Special Equipment*, pp. 26ff.

lxxxvi S-3 Journal, 3d Armored Group.

lxxxvii Jensen, p. 226.

lxxxviii Wilkes, *747th Tank Battalion*, pp. 44, 58.

lxxxix *Armored Special Equipment*, pp. 26ff.

xc Pacific Warfare Board Report No. 74, 26 October 1945, NARA, RG 94, 4-7.74/45, box 24464.

xci Pacific Warfare Board Report No. 66, 9 September 1945, NARA, RG 94, 4-7.60/45, box 24464.

xcii Pacific Warfare Board Report No. 76, 6 November 1945, NARA, RG 94, 4-7.76/45, box 24464. Pacific Warfare Board Report No. 74, 26 October 1945, NARA, RG 94, 4-7.74/45, box 24464.

xciii The 11th Armored Division Association, www.11tharmoreddivision.com,history/713_flame_throwing_tank.html, as of April 2004.

xciv Peter Chamberlain and Chris Ellis. *Pictorial History of Tanks of the World 1915-45* (Harrisburg, Pennsylvania: Stackpole Books, 1972), p. 182.

xcv Belton Y. Cooper, *Death Traps: The Survival of an American Armored Division in World War II* (Novato, Ca: Presidio Press, Inc., 2000), 229-230.

xcvi *Armored Special Equipment*, pp. 4ff.

xcvii *Armored Special Equipment*, pp. 4ff.

xcviii Belton Y. Cooper, *Death Traps: The Survival of an American Armored Division in World War II* (Novato, Ca: Presidio Press, Inc., 2000), 147.

xcix Brigadier Nigel Duncan, "Flail Tanks," *Armored Cavalry Journal*, November-December 1946, 51.

c AARs, 702d and 743d Tank Battalions; *Armored Special Equipment*, 41.

ci AAR for February 1945 and S-3 Journal for March 1945, 737th Tank Battalion.

cii *Armored Special Equipment*, 35-38. Eddie Maddox Jr. *736 Special Tank Battalion* (self-published, 2000), 111 ff. (Hereinafter Maddox.)

ciii Maddox, 77. Date corrected per AAR, 738th Medium Tank Battalion Special (Mine Exploder).

Endnotes for Chapter 6: Assault Guns

civ Memorandum from Gen. Jacob L. Devers, Chief, Army Field Forces, to Maj. Gen. E.S. Hughes, Chief of Ordnance, not dated, NARA, RG 337, Army Field Forces Headquarters, Box 9, folder 470.8.

cv Jim Mesko, *M3 Half-tracks in Action* (Carrollton, Texas: Squadron/Signal Publications, Inc., 1996), np.

cvi Memorandum, "Reports on Combat Experience and Battle Lessons for Training Purposes," Headquarters, 1st Armored Regiment, 9 June 1943, NARA, RG 94, Box 14926.

cvii Lt. Col. George Rubel, *Daredevil Tankers: The Story of the 740th Tank Battalion, United States Army* (Göttingen, Germany: 740th Tank Battalion, 1945), 245.

cviii Armored Force Board report 343, 10 March 1943, NARA, RG 156, Chief of Ordnance, Box J-363.

cix *Tank Gunnery*, The General Board, United States Forces, European Theater, not dated.

cx Lt. Col. George Rubel, *Daredevil Tankers: The Story of the 740th Tank Battalion, United States Army* (Göttingen, Germany: 740th Tank Battalion, 1945), 253.

cxi AAR, 746th Tank Battalion, for January 1945.

Endnotes for Chapter 7: Tank Crew

cxii Homer D. Wilkes, *APO 230* (Scottsdale, Arizona: self-published, 1982), 80.

cxiii Lt. Col. George Rubel, *Daredevil Tankers: The Story of the 740th Tank Battalion, United States Army* (Göttingen, Germany: 740th Tank Battalion, 1945), 241.

cxiv Pacific Warfare Board Report No. 66, 9 September 1945, NARA, RG 94, 4-7.60/45, box 24464.

cxv Armored Force Board reports 136-20, 15 December 1942; 136-21, 20 February 1943; 136-15, 12 March 1943; 136-27, 12 January 1944; 136-38, 136-31, 27 January 1944; 1 November 1944; all NARA, RG 156, Chief of Ordnance, Box J-358.

cxvi Lt. Col. George Rubel, *Daredevil Tankers: The Story of the 740th Tank Battalion, United States Army* (Göttingen, Germany: 740th Tank Battalion, 1945), 92-93.

cxvii Pacific Warfare Board Report No. 66, 9 September 1945, NARA, RG 94, 4-7.60/45, box 24464. Pacific Warfare Board Report No. 72, 16 October 1945, NARA, RG 94, 4-7.72/45, box 24464.

cxviii *Tank Gunnery*, The General Board, United States Forces, European Theater, not dated.

cxix MacDonald, *The Battle of the Bulge*, 62.

cxx Pacific Warfare Board Report No. 74, 26 October 1945, NARA, RG 94, 4-7.74/45, box 24464.

cxxi Charles Palmer, interview with author, April 2004. AAR, Ryukus Operation, and historical report 718th Amphibian Tractor Battalion.

cxxii Belton Y. Cooper,

Index

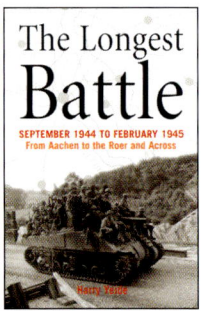

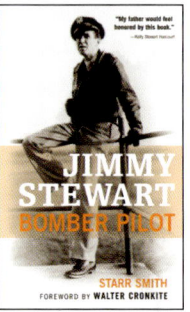
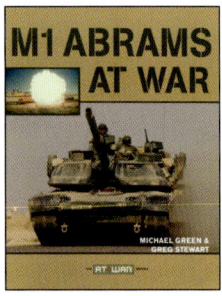
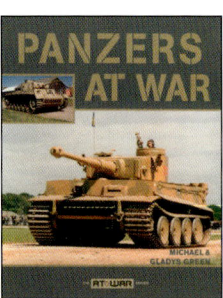
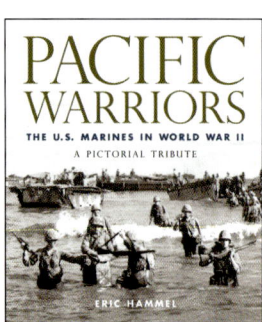

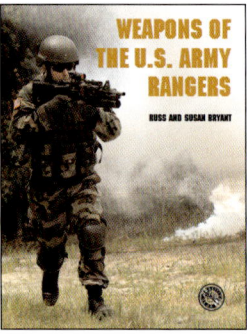
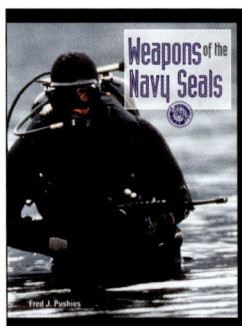